THE ROCKWELL INTERNATIONAL B-1A/B STORY

The prototype B-1A, 74-0158, is seen being rolled out of final assembly and from there into the paint shop, at Rockwell's Air Force Plant 42 at Palmdale, California, shortly before the official roll-out ceremony on October 26, 1974. Prior to painting, 74-0158, had undergone a series of ground vibration tests to verify the structural integrity criteria that had been developed earlier using computer models. The extended spoilers and wing root section fairing details are noteworthy.

CREDITS:

Aerofax, Inc. and the authors are indebted to Col. James Abbee, Tom Brewer, Richard Dunne and Rich Palmee of AIL/Eaton Corp., Maj. Ron Hinkel of the ASD/SPO B-1B, the Boeing Military Airplane Company, René Francillon, Ph.D., James Behmer of Cleveland Pneumatic, Edwards AFB historian Richard Hallion, Ph.D., James Goodall, Henry Ham, Editor John W. R. Taylor of *Jane's All The World's Aircraft*, Dennis Jenkins, Craig Kaston (special thanks), Gayle Lawson, Mike McCary, John Brooks of McDonnell Douglas Corp., Robert Grill and Pat McDowell of Menasco/Colt Industries, Susan Miller, David Morgan, David Blankenship and Mike Matthews of Rockwell International, Brian Rogers, Mick Roth, Edward Seay, Jr., Director Walter Boyne of the Smithsonian Institution's National Air & Space Museum, Maj. Bob Sutton, C. L. "Nick" Taylor of Vought Aero Products Division, Barbara Wasson, and Richard King of Westinghouse Electric Corporation.

PROGRAM HISTORY:

The U.S. Air Force and its predecessor services have long been of the conviction that a heavy bomber deterrent force is an integral element in the proclaimed U.S. objective to maintain world peace. Large U.S. heavy bomber forces reached their numerical peak during the latter stages of World War II, having suffered through many years of neglect during the preceeding quarter-century, and by the end of the 1940's decade, they were considered the single most important military vehicle for the delivery of powerful weapons over intercontinental ranges.

Post-war bomber design and development was maintained at a surprisingly high level, but production funding was curtailed in order to accommodate the rather severe postwar economic slump. Serious inter-service rivalry, the end product of recession-era funding constraints, developed between the Air Force and Navy, these centering on which service had responsibility for strategic deterrence. Navy arguments stemmed from their firm belief that carrier-borne bombers strategically placed on the world's oceans around the globe could more quickly deliver nuclear weapons to target areas than conventional bombers based in the continental United States. The Air Force countered with the argument that carriers were exceptionally vulnerable to aircraft and submarine attack, and carrier-borne bombers were of necessity too small to carry a legitimate payload.

Though neither service, by the mid-1950's, had emerged from the strategic weapons delivery argument unquestionably victorious, the fact remained that heavy funding emphasis had shifted in favor of USAF strategic medium and heavy bombers; this tactfully underscoring the fact that the responsibility for strategic nuclear weapons delivery had quietly fallen on the USAF side of the fence.

The most important US heavy bomber to emerge from the postwar period was unquestionably Boeing's B-52 *Stratofortress*. Essentially a design offshoot of the Boeing B-47 *Stratojet*—which was to become perhaps the most successful medium jet bomber in USAF history—it was initiated as the Model 464 design study (under the direction of Boeing engineers Ed Wells, George Schairer, H. W. Withington, Vaughn Blumenthal, Art Carlsen, and Maynard Pennell) in the late 1940's, and was to reach fruition in the form of the first XB-52/Model 464-67 (49-230) which was rolled out in great secrecy during the night of November 29, 1951. Offering the Air Force high performance at altitude, a range of intercontinental dimensions, the attribute of being inflight refuelable, and a payload of extraordinary proportions, it was the first new bomber design to claim a significant performance improvement over the immense, but technologically outdated Convair B-36 *Peacemaker*.

Boeing's successful approach to the design and performance of the B-52 would, in fact, lead to a heavy bomber whose operational career would exceed, by far, the late 1940's prognostications of its creators. Political, economic, and technological anomolies would eventually create a need for the B-52 to remain in front line service for nearly a third of a century. As of the date of this publication, the end of its lengthy career has only recently come into view.

The B-52, of course, was not the only bomber developed during the three decades from 1950 to 1980. In fact, a significant number were prototyped, especially during the 1950's, and on several occasions, production contracts were awarded and executed. Among the more notable examples of the latter were Convair's awesome Mach 2-capable B-58 *Hustler* (116 built) and General Dynamics' somewhat misbegotten FB-111A (76 built). It was for good reason, however, that only the B-52 could lay claim to a significant production run. Simply stated, it was a good airplane that accommodated its mission requirements dependably and as needed.

The successes realized by the B-52 during the late

The full-scale B-1A mock-up was built at Rockwell's facility near Los Angeles International Airport. Constructed primarily of wood, it weighed just over 45,000 lbs. and was left uncovered on its right half to expose for inspection various internal details. The left wing could be swept using a manual system.

The official roll-out of B-1A, 74-0158, took place at Rockwell's Palmdale facility on October 26, 1974. Media coverage of the event was quite thorough.

During the many years it took for the B-1 to reach fruition, a large number of design configurations were explored by Rockwell. Most of these were conducted under the auspices of the various AMPSS and AMPS programs. From left to right the studies include four AMPSS, one Contract Task 7, and one Contract Task 14A.

1950's essentially pacified the Air Force and prevented the service from feeling any desperate need for a replacement intercontinental heavy bomber in the short term. Accordingly, though a variety of advanced bomber design studies were funded, including many for aircraft of improved high-altitude and low-altitude performance, greater range, and improved payload capacity, the continuing improvement in capability provided the B-52 family through uprated and improved propulsion systems and miscellaneous systems modifications continued to dull any urgency the Air Force might feel to develop a replacement.

Additionally, though the ''Red Menace'' was often touted as rationale for funding new intercontinental bombers, the steadily improving dependability and accuracy of the USAF's and Navy's intercontinental, intermediate, and submarine launched ballistic missile fleets muffled what little vociferous support any new bomber program might have garnered. There was, in fact, a general feeling that the day of the manned bomber had reached its zenith with the B-52 and that a follow-on aircraft was not likely to reach the hardware stage in light of intercontinental range missile development and noted improvements in Soviet surface-to-air missiles.

Perhaps the only serious attempt during this period to develop a B-52 replacement was North American's exotic WS-110A/XB-70A supersonic intercontinental heavy bomber. This was to be a short-lived program, however, as technological difficulties, its design optimization for high-altitude penetration, Soviet anti-aircraft capabilities, and extraordinary cost overruns, effectively killed the program after the completion of two prototypes (62-0001 and 62-0207) and an only partially successful flight test program.

By the late 1950's, some of the sentiment in favor of the ICBM had begun to wane and the concept of the ''Triad'' approach to the nuclear deterrent issue, in which manned bombers, land-based ICBM's, and submarines made up the retaliatory element of the U.S. military posture, began to take shape. As the ''Triad'' philosophy gained support, so did a renewed Air Force and DoD interest in the manned bomber program. The argument was basically in favor of having at least one ''flexible 'Triad' leg''—and a manned bomber, because it could be recalled even after a mission was started, was the only feasible option available.

By this time, the B-52 was reaching the end of its first decade of service. Though the B-52 fleet was not yet showing any physical signs of aging, it had become apparent that the mission profile around which it had been designed (high altitude penetration) was no longer viable. On May 1, 1960, Francis Gary Powers penetrated Soviet airspace at an altitude of over 70,000 feet in a Central Intelligence Agency Lockheed U-2 equipped with the most advanced electronic countermeasures equipment then known, and was shot down by a shotgun launch of SAM-2 missiles.

The loss of Powers' aircraft led not only to major political repercussions world wide, but also to a major realignment of U.S. military strategy. It was now undeniable that Soviet anti-aircraft equipment and techniques could be effective against high-altitude aircraft.

With the Powers' event sending shock waves throughout DoD and the intelligence community, a major realignment of various programs began to take place. among the many affected were those that had been initiated to accommodate SAC's still-evolving requirement for a B-52 replacement. High-altitude penetration capability was no longer a priority; low-altitude penetration was . . .

The first requirements for the advanced bomber study that would eventually lead to the Rockwell International B-1 as a replacement for the B-52 were identified during 1960 and 1961. These requirements and definition studies were actually consummated during 1962 by two separate study groups, *Project Forecast* and a general officer panel. These two groups concluded, independently, that a replacement bomber was indeed needed, and that its capabilities must provide the Air Force with significant versatility and greatly improved weapons delivery capability.

Many studies were conducted to refine these requirements and to provide solutions to possible development risks that had been identified. Some of the studies and their associated acronyms were Subsonic Low Altitude Bomber (SLAB) in 1961; Extended Range Strike Aircraft (ERSA) in 1963; Advanced Manned Precision Strike System (AMPSS) in 1964; and Advanced Manned Strategic Aircraft (AMSA) in 1965.

AMPSS became the first study to define the elements that would eventually dictate the design and mission objectives of the pivotal AMSA program. AMPSS called for preliminary design and evaluation of economic technical feasibility of four aircraft concepts: (1) all subsonic low altitude; (2) subsonic low altitude with high altitude medium supersonic capability; (3) subsonic low altitude with a high altitude, high supersonic capability; and (4) vertical/short takeoff and landing capability.

The AMPSS studies ended in 1965 and were followed later in the year by the AMSA studies which continued into early 1969. The AMSA program called for five supplementary studies: (1) a propulsion study; (2) an alternate armament loading study; (3) a reliability study; (4) a titanium cost study; and (5) a maintainability study. Within the AMSA studies were a long list of separate study tasks, such as crew factors, limited war analysis, enduring survivability, survivability and vulnerability, design trade studies, and bomber decoy missile analysis.

As a result of these studies and the numerous peripheral studies that took place under their auspices, every area of high risk was identified and thoroughly examined in detail. Additionally, essential advanced development was accomplished in many areas, and in some cases, ''brass board'' equipment was prototyped and flight tested.

As mentioned previously, the loss of Powers' U-2B was one of the key elements considered by the various study groups tasked with putting together the various requirements calling for a B-52 replacement.

The loss of Powers' aircraft destroyed the high altitude penetration philosophy forever, and as a result, almost all programs calling for the development of high-altitude penetrators were terminated, and great emphasis was placed on developing aircraft that could operate continuously at or near sea level.

The B-1 was born out of the last of the aforementioned B-52 replacement studies, the Advanced Manned Strategic Aircraft project. Funded during 1965, AMSA took four years to execute. Finally, on November 3, 1969, it led to the release to interested bidders of the official B-1 Request for Proposal (RFP).

By the time of the RFP's unveiling, many major aerospace manufacturers had been involved in B-52 follow-on aircraft design studies for, in some cases, nearly two decades. The three airframe manufacturers who now became the most serious contract contenders were Boeing, with their extensive experience in the design and production of heavy bombers; Convair (General Dynamics), with their follow-on B-36 and B-58 studies; and Rockwell International (North American), with their on-going post-XB-70 efforts. Additionally, the two major U.S. powerplant manufacturers, Pratt & Whitney and General Electric, also submitted responses.

Just over six months later, on June 5, 1970, Rockwell International's Los Angeles, California division was awarded research, development, test, and evaluation contracts for the B-1 airframe, and General Electric was picked over Pratt & Whitney to undertake similar studies for their proposed F101 turbofan engine.

The original cost-plus-incentive contracts called for five flying prototype B-1's, two structural test airframes, and 40 test and evaluation engines. By January, 1971, when the basic design parameters of the B-1 had been frozen, cost constraints had led to the elimination of two of the flight test aircraft, one of the structural test aircraft, and 13 of the engines. Later, budgeting for one of the flight test aircraft was restored under the FY 1976 budget.

This initial contract agreement called for the delivery of the first aircraft during early 1975 and the delivery of the final production aircraft during 1981. A total of 244 B-1's were then on order, with 240 of these operationally configured. Over-all, the B-1 program was then expected to generate a total of 192,000 jobs, nation-wide.

Following final approval of the 45,000 lb. full-scale mock-up (construction of which had begun during January, 1971, utilizing some 150 Rockwell employees) on November 4, 1971 (the actual review had taken place from October 18 through October 31; this resulted in 297 requests for alteration, of which 257 were resolved on the spot), assembly of the prototype B-1, 74-0158, using major sub-assemblies from Rockwell's Los Angeles division and the numerous sub-contractors scattered around the

U.S., was begun at Rockwell's Palmdale, California facility (Air Force Plant 42) on March 15, 1972. Concurrently, an extensive wind tunnel test program, which would eventually result in over 22,000 hours of wind tunnel time, remained on-going under the auspices of Rockwell and the Air Force, and peripheral work exploring radar cross section and other related parameters took place at various facilities around the U.S. The latter tests included the construction of a full-scale B-1 breadboard target vehicle and a 3,300 lb. 36' long RCS model (tested at the USAF's Radar Target Scatter Facility at Holloman AFB, New Mexico).

All four B-1 prototypes were now assembled in wide-spaced succession, with the first being completed just over two years after initiation of construction. In front of a crowd of nearly 10,000 people, this aircraft (74-0158) was rolled out at Palmdale on October 26, 1974, and following an extensive ground test program, was flown for the first time on December 23 (the crew consisted of pilot Charles Bock, Jr., co-pilot Col. Emil Sturmthal, and flight test engineer Richard Abrams). This flight also marked the first flight for the General Electric YF101. A second flight, taking place on January 23, 1975, became the first in which the landing gear was retracted and the wing sweep mechanism was activated.

Following roll out on January 16, 1976, the third B-1, 74-0160, became the second to fly (the second B-1, 74-0159, was then being utilized at Lockheed's Palmdale facility as a structural test airframe, thus delaying its first flight date) when it took to the air from the Palmdale facility on April 1. Less than two months later, and following its roll out on May 11, 1976, the second B-1, 74-0159, became airborne for the first time on June 14. Finally, on February 14, 1979, the fourth and last of the prototype aircraft, 76-0174, which had entered production on August 25, 1975, made its first flight.

Each of the four prototypes had been assigned various flight test responsibilities prior to its completion. Aircraft 74-0158 was to evaluate flying qualities over a flight test program that eventually totaled 79 flights (logging 405 hrs. 18 min.; this aircraft also became the first B-1 to reach Mach 1.5, achieving this speed during October, 1975, and also the first to reach Mach 2, achieving this speed during April, 1976); aircraft 74-0159 was to evaluate structural loading parameters (it eventually completed 60 flights and logged 282 hrs. 30 min. while accommodating the data gathering process; it also logged the highest speed attained by any B-1, this being Mach 2.22 achieved on October 5, 1978); aircraft 74-0160 was used as an offensive and defensive weapons systems testbed (by April 30, 1981, when the test program originally authorized ended, this had resulted in 138 flights and 829 hrs. 24 min. flight time); and aircraft 76-0174, which also accommodated the offensive and defensive systems test program though integrating systems that were effectively operational in configuration (this aircraft, also affected by the April 30, 1981 deadline, completed 70 missions for a total of 378 hours flight time).

Phase I flight testing was completed on schedule by September 30, 1976, and the DoD and USAF announced on December 2, that the first production contracts had been placed calling for the construction of the first three operational aircraft and the purchase of long-lead items for the second lot of eight operational aircraft. Additionally, funds were authorized for the purchase and fabrication of production tooling.

B-1 appropriations for production aircraft had, in fact, been allocated under the FY 1978 budget during the final year of the Ford administration and it was therefore with great effort and extraordinary political maneuvering that the succeeding Carter administration, on June 30, 1977, took the unprecedented step of cancelling the program almost in its entirety. This act was the end result of many elements, not the least of which was an unsympathetic public that was suffering through a major shift in the nation's economic stance, and an Air Force budget that was being stretched to its limits by many programs of extraordinary expense and magnitude. These factors, coupled with the rapid and relatively successful development of cruise missile technology and hardware, and a DoD that privately maintained mixed emotions concerning the need for a manned, long-range weapons delivery system, gave Carter the incentive he needed to terminate the immense Rockwell contract.

Though the B-1 program was now effectively gutted, flight testing using the third and fourth prototypes (74-0160 and 76-0174, respectively) continued. The third prototype had been equipped with an advanced electronic countermeasures system and a Doppler beam-sharpening modification to the forward-looking attack radar, and the fourth prototype had been equipped with the aforementioned operationally-configured defensive avionics system. It was thus considered appropriate for research purposes that tests relating to these sytems should be continued—even though the B-1 program had officially ended.

Though the B-1 was now considered dead, ongoing evolutionary studies were continued at Rockwell to explore potential design improvements and to incorporate miscellaneous advances in equipment and technology. Additionally, and perhaps most importantly, a requirement began to evolve within DoD calling for an aircraft that could be used to replace the B-52 as a cruise missile transport.

During 1978, the cruise-missile-carrying B-1 concept was submitted to the DoD for consideration in an industry-wide request for proposals. During November, 1979, as a result of these studies, Rockwell was requested by the Air Force to submit a more defined proposal calling for the initial planning and design effort associated with a B-1 "core aircraft" derivative flight demonstration prototype using the third B-1, 74-0160, as a flight test demonstrator. Shortly thereafter it was identified as a strategic air launched cruise missile launcher under the acronym SAL (further acronyms would eventually be applied including CMCA-Cruise Missile Carrier Aircraft; LRCA-Long Range Cruise Aircraft; MRB-Multi-Role Bomber; NTP-Near-Term Penetrator; and SWL-Strategic Weapons Launcher).

While work on the SAL-configured B-1 studies was undertaken at DoD, Rockwell continued an on-going study of various B-1 derivatives that could be manufactured at reduced cost while providing expanded mission roles as priorities. Simultaneously, DoD initiated a study through the Air Force Scientific Advisory Board that was tasked with determining the direction of future bomber development. The board concluded that the next bomber should be a multi-disciplined design, capable of undertaking a variety of missions, and that it should not be developed only to carry cruise missiles or to deliver free-falling thermonuclear weapons. Additionally, the board noted that the proposed Rockwell B-1 derivative study offered the best over-all design for an aircraft that could accomplish, with an IOC (initial operational capability) in 1987, missions outlined in the board's recommendation.

While the DoD and U.S. Congress, in early 1981, continued deliberating the budget elements that would dictate the possible revival of the B-1 in a redefined form, the last flight of the original prototype program, utilizing B-1, 76-0174, took place at Edwards AFB, on April 30. This aircraft was now moved into storage alongside the other three prototypes, and left to wait for future developments.

On October 2, 1981, following the receipt and analysis of the Air Force's recommendation that the service select the Long Range Combat Aircraft (LRCA) version of the B-1 over the stretched General Dynamics FB-111H, newly-elected President Reagan, long a proponent of the manned bomber and politically motivated by the fact the Rockwell International B-1 production facilities were located in his home state of California, announced that the USAF would be cleared to order some 100 B-1 derivatives under the new designation, B-1B. Consequent to the latter, the four prototype B-1's, including 74-0158 and 74-0159 in storage, and 74-0160 and 76-0174 still considered flightworthy, were retroactively and officially redesignated B-1A.

On January 20, 1982, Rockwell and the Air Force signed two flight test and production contracts. The first of these was a $1,317,000,000 full-scale development agreement which required Rockwell to finalize the B-1B design and modify and flight test 74-0159 and 76-0174 as B-1B prototypes; and the second was an $886,000,000 production contract covering the construction of the first production B-1B and procurement of long-lead items for early production lots. Concurrently, the Air Force also granted a contract to General Electric for construction of initial production batches of the F100-GE-102 engine (a total of 469 engines have now been ordered, including 400 installed and 69 as spares). The first of these for the

B-1A, 74-0158, in landing configuration at Edwards AFB. The full-span leading edge slats can be seen in their extended position. Particularly noteworthy are the closed main gear well doors which cycle as the gear extend and retract.

Rear view looking forward of B-1A, 74-0158. Aerodynamic cleanliness of aircraft undersurfaces is readily apparent, as is large size of horizontal stabilator. Noteworthy are engine exhaust nozzles in cruise thrust position.

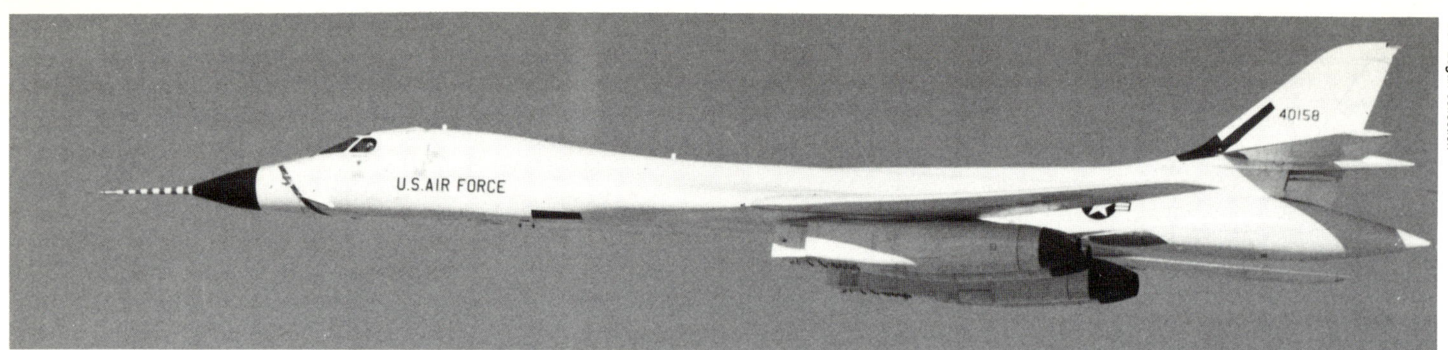

B-1A, 74-0158, in level flight over Edwards AFB, with wings in maximum sweep position. As a testbed, this aircraft was equipped with very few operationally configured systems, and was instead, heavily instrumented. One of the most distinctive external features was its sizable nose test boom, used primarily for flight instrument calibration requirements. The all-white paint scheme was particularly appropriate for the hot desert environment of Edwards AFB.

first production B-1B was delivered on September 30, 1983. These contracts were expected to generate work for some 3,000 companies and require the employment of some 58,000 people (including 22,000 for Rockwell).

General Electric's contract with the Air Force also provides for integrated logistics support (ILS), which incorporates all of the elements required to maintain the engine at its operating base. Included are a training engine, spare parts, technical orders, operational support equipment, and a comprehensive engine management system. ILS will be implemented at all bases with B-1B aircraft, as well as the Oklahoma City Air Logistics Center, Oklahoma City, Oklahoma.

Modification of B-1A, 74-0159, incorporating many B-1B subsystems (mainly flight controls), took Rockwell just over a year to complete. On March 23, 1983, it took to the air (from Edwards AFB) for the first time following modification, beginning a long-term program designed to explore the various systems updates and also to undertake a flight envelope expansion program covering stability, control, and flutter. Additionally, it was to be used for various weapons release and separation tests.

Unfortunately, manual fuel management difficulties coupled with the fact that the aircraft was operating in a low-altitude environment, thus precluding any chance for recovery, caused 74-0159 to crash at Edwards AFB, California, on August 29, 1984, killing Rockwell test pilot Doug Benefield, and causing serious injury to Maj. Richard Reynolds, the pilot, and to Captain Otto Waniczek, the acting flight test engineer. This accident led to a number of changes in the B-1B's fuel management system, the majority of which will be incorporated in the B-1B production program beginning with aircraft number 19.

On July 30, 1984, B-1A, 76-0174, also took to the air (from Edwards AFB) for the first time since modification, now equipped with the full B-1B offensive and defensive avionics systems not found on 74-0159. Additionally, this aircraft, with the exception of its powerplant intakes and associated nacelles, was aerodynamically more similar in configuration to the B-1B than any of the other prototypes.

While B-1B-related flight test work with the two prototype B-1A's got underway at Edwards AFB, the first production B1-B's were beginning to take shape at Rockwell's Palmdale facility (the final assembly station for the latter is 660' by 400' in unobstructed expanse and 73' high; it can accomodate nine B-1B's in section—five in fuselage mate, two in aircraft mate, and two in final assembly; assembled aircraft are moved to an adjacent 254,000 sq.' checkout building capable of housing up to

four B-1B's). The first production B-1B, 82-0001 (coincidentally, the first B-52A was 52-0001, and the first XB-70A was 62-0001), originally scheduled to fly during March, 1985, rolled out some five months ahead of schedule on September 4, 1984, and on October 18, became airborne for the first time (the crew consisted of pilot M. L. Evenson, co-pilot LTC. L. B. Schroeder, DSO Capt. D. E. Hamilton, and OSO Maj. S. A. Henry. The first flight went relatively smoothly, with the aircraft leaving the Palmdale airport at 2:38 p.m. PDT and flying for 3 hrs. 20 min. before landing at Edwards AFB.

The following is a "quick look report" describing the first flight of the B-1B: "The first flight of aircraft B-1B-1 was successfully accomplished on 10-18-84. Following two delays, takeoff occurred at 1438 PDT. All planned avionics systems were operating at takeoff. The primary objectives of the flight were to evaluate flying qualities of the aircraft and assess inflight operation of avionics systems. The aircraft was flown to the Edwards area and all testing was conducted in this region. The entire avionics system operated as expected throughout the flight with the exception of the radar. The radar was turned on approximately ten minutes following takeoff and locked up forty minutes later. The ABDAS digital recorder malfunctioned approximately one hour after takeoff. Several corrective action procedures were attempted but did not fix the malfunction. Serial data indications looked good. The briefed radar workaround procedures were attempted to no avail. The IKB backup was also unsuccessful. Approximately thirty minutes later, radar power came back on without any operator function, with TFACU #1 and PSP/RDT-1 displayed. Even though the radar "ready" light was on, the "cont" and map refresh were not functional. Radar #2 was not selectable. At this point, the decision was made not to pursue further radar tests but to concentrate on aircraft related tests. Defensive avionics "receive only" tests were accomplished using the mutes system. Activity lights were present and the defensive system capability appeared to be compatible with aircraft #4's system. Throughout the flight, various avionics tests were conducted. The INU's worked very well and all central ACC's functioned satisfactorily. The crew was very pleased with the overall avionics performance during the 3.3 hour flight."

During 1982, a committment had been made by DoD to acquire production batches of the B-1B, the first of these, calling for 7 production aircraft, being funded under the FY 1983 budget. An additional 10 followed under the FY 1984 budget, 34 under the FY 1985 budget, and the remaining 48 of the requested 100 following under the FY 1986 budget. As of the first quarter, 1986,

some eight B-1B's had been delivered to the USAF, with scheduled deliveries taking place at an eventual peak rate of four aircraft per month throughout 1986, 1987, and 1988. The last production aircraft is now scheduled for delivery to SAC during July/August, 1988. By that time, a total of $28,500,000,000 (in 1988 dollars) is expected to have been spent.

Following its first flight, the first production B-1B, 82-0001, was assigned permanently to the B-1 combined test force (CTF) at Edwards AFB. However, when 83-0065 was temporarily grounded at Offutt AFB, Nebraska, on June 27, 1985, just prior to SAC acceptance ceremonies there (a flapper door came apart in flight allowing hardware to be ingested by the engine ducts), 82-0001 (flown by Gen. Bennie Davis) was utilized on June 29 (thirty years to the day after delivery of the first B-52, which was turned over to SAC on June 29, 1955, at Castle AFB, California), as a surrogate during the acceptance ceremonies at Dyess AFB. Following the arrival at Dyess AFB of 83-0065 on July 7 (where it was turned over to the 4018th CCTS/96th BW), 82-0001 was returned to Edwards.

Presently, four wings are scheduled to be assigned the B-1B. These include the 96th Bomb Wing at Dyess AFB, Abilene, Texas (to receive 29 aircraft); the 28th Bomb Wing at Ellsworth AFB, Rapid City, South Dakota (35 aircraft); the 319th Bomb Wing at Grand Forks AFB, Grand Forks, North Dakota (17 aircraft); and the 384th Air Refueling Wing (which will be converted to the 384th Bomb Wing when B-1's arrive) at McConnell AFB, Wichita, Kansas (17 aircraft). It has also been mentioned that Otis AFB, near Cape Cod, Massachusetts, will serve as a detachment base for three dedicated maritime surveillance B-1B's. Additionally, the CTF at Edwards AFB will maintain the first and ninth B-1B's for flight test work, and probably the fourth B-1A, as well. As of September, 1985, the entire B-1 fleet, including both B-1A's and B-1B's, had logged over 2,300 hours of flight time.

Follow-on B-1B production programs and advanced designs are, of course, presently being discussed. Production contracts beyond those currently in effect are likely to be seriously affected by the Air Force's on-going infatuation with low observability, or "stealth" technology and the continuing development and eventual flight test of Northrop's all-wing Advanced Technology Bomber (ATB). The latter is scheduled for rollout during 1988, and its performance and overall success as a bomber will be highly dependent upon how well it meets the primary criterion of low radar cross section.

Little information has leaked out concerning advanced B-1 design studies, but it can be safely assumed that such aircraft, if ever they reach the hardware stage, will be optimized for even lower radar cross section than the B-1A/B, and improved performance. Many options are available to Rockwell, including increased gross weights, fuselage stretches, avionics updates, and powerplant changes. The airframe, for instance, is technically a supersonic design, though it is Mach limited by its intake configuration. A redesign of the latter, coupled with minor control systems adjustments, could quickly convert the B-1B to a supersonic bombing platform.

Several early B-1 studies have recently come to light, though little has been revealed concerning them. B-1C, B-1D, and B-1E designators have apparently been applied to some of these, though only the B-1E has been defined. The B-1E was optimized for use by the Navy, and was essentially an escort configuration capable of carrying a very large number of Hughes AIM-54 *Phoenix* air-to-air missiles.

Following cancellation of the B-1A in 1977, Rockwell

With its wings in their fully swept position, B-1A, 74-0158, is seen during a test flight over Edwards AFB. Wing sweep, which is actuated by a simple hydraulic motor-driven screw-jack system, is manually chosen by the crew using actuation handles mounted on the two cockpit wall consoles.

unveiled a number of proposals for austere B-1 configurations, these including several with fixed, semi-delta wings and provisions for accommodating sizable external stores loads. With the rebirth of the B-1 program under the auspices of the B-1B designator, these configuration studies were placed on hold, and little else has surfaced concerning them.

Rockwell continues to offer the aircraft for missions other than those identified by the USAF. It is suitable for deployment in a variety of roles now considered optional for the B-52, these including anti-submarine patrol, maritime surveillance over exceptionally long ranges, and aerial minelaying. Interestingly, because of its ability to carry auxiliary fuel tanks in its weapons bays, it has also been proffered as a long range high speed inflight refueling tanker.

CONSTRUCTION AND SYSTEMS:

The B-1A and B-1B are dedicated long range strategic bombers optimized for low altitude penetration of unfriendly airspace. The B-1A, because of its limited production run, is now relegated to the flight test role only and utilized sparingly as a testbed for the B-1B. There are many physical and performance differences between the B-1A and B-1B, and these are covered in greater detail elsewhere in this section. Basically, however, the B-1A is somewhat lighter than its successor, and is equipped with significantly fewer state-of-the-art primary and secondary subsystems. Additionally, the B-1A's F101 engines are considered pre-production configurations and thus are not as reliable or as efficient as their production counterparts.

More than 60% of the structure of the B-1B is subcontracted, with some 3,000 subcontractors and suppliers being involved in the program. Major subcontractors include the following: Aeronca (engine shrouds); AIL/Eaton (defensive avionics); AiResearch (central air data computer and weapons bay door drives); Avco (wings); Bendix (radomes); Boeing (offensive avionics); Chemtronics (augmentor case and ducts); Cleveland Pneumatic (main landing gear); Crane Hydro-Aire (anti-skid subsystem); Garrett Turbine Engine Co. (secondary power systems); General Electric (engine thrust control, engine instruments, powerplant); B. F. Goodrich (tires); Goodyear (wheels and brakes, windows); Hamilton Standard (environmental control systems); Harris (electrical multiplex); Heath (tail warning radome); Hughes Treitler (heat exchangers); IBM (computer control unit and memory); Inco Alloys (MAC-54 alloy); Kaman (engine access doors, rudder, and horizontal actuator fairing); Kelsey-Hayes (flap/slat actuator subsystem and rotary launcher drive); Kuras-Alterman (ECM); MAL Tool (stage 2 fan blades); Martin Marietta (horizontal and vertical stabilizers and structural mode control vanes); Menasco (nose landing gear shock strut); Northrop (jamming transmitters); Parker Hannifin (fuel injector and augmentor); Raytheon (phased-array antenna); Sanders (electrical display unit); Sierracin (aft crew windows and windscreens); Simmonds Precision (fuel center of gravity management system); SEDCO (RF antennas); Singer Kearfott (flight instrument signal converter and multiplex interface module); Sperry (automatic flight control and gyro stabilization, vertical situation displays); Sperry-Vickers (emergency electrical power system and primary hydraulic pumps); SSP Products (engine bleed air ducts); Sterer Engineering (steering and damping subsystem); Sundstrand (constant speed drive, engine bleed air controls, rudder controls, and wing sweep system); Swedlow (windscreens); Systron Donner (flight control inertial subsystems); Telephonics (central integrated test system); TRW (fuel pumps and turbine blades); UNC Tech Products (fan stator case); United Aircraft Products (precooler/heat exchangers); Vicars (fuel pumps); Vought Aero Products (aft and intermediate aft fuselage); Weber Aircraft (ejection seats); Western Gear Corp. (engine accessory gearboxes); Westinghouse Electric (generator and controls); Woodville Polymer (wing fairing seal system); Woodward Governor (main engine control); and Wyman Gordon (stage 2 HPT disk).

The structure of the B-1B utilizes principally aluminum alloys, composites, and titanium, and is hardened to withstand the extremes of nuclear radiation and blast overpressure. The external shell of the aircraft, through the liberal use of compound curves and composites, is optimized to lower its radar cross-section (RCS). This, coupled with one of the most advanced ECM systems in the world, gives the B-1B an RCS that is 1/100th that

The aft fuselage section for the first B-1A, 74-0158, constructed primarily of titanium, is shown just after it was moved out of its assembly facility at Palmdale. Vought Aero Products Division now builds similar assemblies for the B-1B program.

Much of the forward fuselage intermediate section and wing carry-through section (with wing hinge assemblies in place) for the first B-1A, 74-0158, is seen undergoing assembly inside Rockwell's Palmdale facility. This unit contains most of the B-1A's internal fuel tankage as well as its three bomb bays.

The first set of moveable outer wing panels for the first B-1A, 74-0158, are seen in their jigs at Rockwell's Palmdale facility. The hinged, inboard ends of the wings where they will be attached to the wing carry-through section are visible to the left. The pivot lugs are made of double plate titanium.

The first two B-1A's, 74-0158 (rear) and 74-0159, are seen in Rockwell's final assembly building at Palmdale. Visible are pieces of the fuselage jig structure. The vertical fin, wings, horizontal stabilizers, and nose cone have yet to be attached to 74-0159.

of the Boeing B-52.

The fuselage is a conventional, area ruled, fail safe, stressed-skin design of closely spaced frames and longerons, built primarily of 2025 and 7075 aluminum alloys. It is made up of five main sections comprising forward, forward intermediate, wing carry-through, rear intermediate, and rear fuselage assemblies. Titanium is used for the tail support structure, the rear fuselage skins and other high load or high heat areas (such as the engine bays and firewalls). The dorsal spine is of steel/boron filled titanium sandwich construction. The nose radome is of polyimide quartz and all fuselage dielectric panels are of fiberglass. The small structural mode control system (SMCS) vanes located on either side of the nose, just to the rear of the nose radome are of composite material and mounted with 30° of anhedral.

The B-1B's pressurized cockpit, which is accessed through a under-fuselage mounted hatch and retractable ladder located just aft of the nose landing gear, contains a crew of four consisting of a pilot, a co-pilot, an offensive systems officer (OSO), and a defensive systems officer (DSO). All four crew members are seated on Weberbuilt (McDonnell Douglas designed) ACES II (Advanced Concept Ejection Seat) ejection seats which are zero-zero capable and which eject vertically through egress ports left by dorsal hatches which automatically jettison when the ejection sequence is initiated.

The B-1B ACES II seat is similar to that found in the F-15 and other aircraft, but differs in having armrests (which are now expected to be removed), a comfort cushion, and an upper torso webbing restraint system which deploys automatically during the ejection sequence. Each seat incorporates a personal parachute and emergency oxygen supply for its respective crew member. The seat has three recovery modes which are automatic functions depending on the airspeed and altitude at which ejection occurs.

Because there is no ejectable accommodation for unseated instructor personnel (two folding seats only), personal parachutes only are provided for emergency egress. Bailout for the instructors is accommodated through the crew entry ladder well.

The first three B-1A's were equipped with an encapsulated ejection system called a crew escape module that provided the crew with a shirtsleeve ejection environment in an emergency. This unit was first sled tested at Holloman AFB, New Mexico, on March 29, 1973, when it was boosted to an altitude of over 450' off a mock-up B-1 forward fuselage. The actual module contained its own parachutes (a drogue and three mains) and a pair of rocket motors (one fixed, one gimballed) which generated a total of 60,000 lbs. th. for approximately 1.8 seconds. A gyro positioned the gimballed motor for direction control. The ejection process was initiated by pulling the ejection handles. An energy transfer system (ETS) consisting of a series of lines containing explosive charges and directing devices, removed the module from the forward section of the aircraft. The ETS was purely mechanical and redundant; there were two separate lines for each function routed through different parts of the module. The module could also be utilized as a shelter on both land and water, following ejection. The unit was functional throughout almost all of the B-1A's flight envelope.

The B-1 cabin area is divided into two primary station areas, with the pilot and co-pilot seated side-by-side (front), and the defensive systems officer (left) and offensive systems officer (right) sitting side-by-side (aft). All four crew members face forward. Crew cabin oxygen is generated by an onboard Molecular Sieve Oxygen Generating System (MSOGS) which uses engine bleed air to supply breathing oxygen to each crewmember's oxygen mask. This system is used in place of the conventional LOX system.

The flight panel consists of a combination of digital and analogue instruments and several CRT's. Aircraft control is accommodated via stick and rudder, much along the lines of contemporary fighter aircraft, though two throttle quadrants are provided (one for the pilot and one for the co-pilot). The DSO and OSO stations are equipped with three multi-function displays (MFD), of which two are at the OSO station and one at the DSO station. These provide the display capability for alpha-numeric data or for radar data as a backup display. The units are identical to those developed for the B-52G/H OAS and provide a 6-1/2'' by 8-1/2'' display area. Contrast, brightness, and self-test controls are provided for individual display adjustment of the video unit. Both stations have integrated keyboards (IKB) which provide the OSO and DSO with the control necessary to perform the following functions: select current MFD (OSO only); control current MFD character brightness; select high level logic tree format; select menu options; manually enter data as required on current format; and control video recorder (OSO only).

The OSO's station, which also serves as a navigational system station, is provided with two sources of navigation data: an inertial navigation system (INS) and a dead reckoning (DR) navigation system. Both systems operate simultaneously with one navigational system designated as primary. The INS utilizes inertial platform data to calculate the navigation paramotors, while the DR system uses gyro stabilization system (GSS), central air data computer (CADC), and Doppler velocity sensor data.

The vertical and horizontal tail surfaces are cantilever fail-safe structures with leading edge sweepback on all surfaces. The fin is a conventional titanium and aluminum alloy torsion box structure, secured to the rear fuselage by a double shear attachment, bolts on the tailplane spindle, a vertical shear pin in the tailplane spindle fitting, and a shear-bolt joint on the front beam of the box. The rudder, which is provided with 25° of travel to either side, is a three section aluminum alloy structure. The two-section all moving horizontal stabilator is operated collectively in pitch (10° up and 25° down) and differentially in roll (20° up and 20° down). The two halves move independently on the steel spindle. The rudder and horizontal stabilators are actuated hydraulically, with a fly-by-wire backup system for use in the event of a mechanical system failure.

The wing is a cantilever fail-safe design that is blended at the root section into the fuselage center section. The wing is of the variable geometry type, with the outer panels being articulated. The wing carry-through structure, which is sealed as an integral fuel tank, is mainly of diffusion bonded 6AL-4V titanium. The wing pivot mechanism is of the same material, with a hinge pin made from a single 6AL-4V forging on each side, in spherical steel bearings, above and below which are integrally stiffened double cover plates of machined titanium. Wing sweep, which is infinitely variable at any angle between 15° and 67.5°, is actuated by screwjacks, driven by four hydraulic motors; sweep can be accomplished using any of two of the aicraft's four hydraulic systems, asymmetric movement being prevented by a torque shaft between the two screwjacks. Sweep actuators are covered by a leading-edge ''knuckle'' fairing which prevents a gap from opening when the outer panels are swept back.

Aft of the wing pivot points are overwing fairings which blend the wing trailing edges and engine nacelles. Each of the wing panels, which have 15° of leading edge sweep when fully forward and 67° 30 min. of sweep when fully swept (wing sweep is *manually* controlled from the cockpit by the wing sweep lever), is a conventional two-spar aluminum alloy torsion box structure, with machined spars, ribs, and one-piece integrally stiffened top and bottom skin panels. The wingtips, wing/body fairings, and some outer wing skin panels, are of fiberglass. Canvas covered inflatable rubber air bladders suffice to fill the gap left at the root section and fuselage fairing points when the wings are swept fully forward.

Full-span seven-segment leading edge slats located on the leading edge of each outer wing panel can be drooped 20° for take-off and landing. Six-segment single-slotted trailing edge Fowler-type flaps with a maximum deployment angle of 40° are located on the trailing edge of each outer wing panel. Movement of the flap/slat control handle past the point which activates the slats causes the flaps to move after slat extension to a position proportional to the handle position. Flap operation is constrained by the wing sweep and slat positions. Flap extension is impossible with a wing sweep angle of greater than 20°. When the wings reach 20°, an interlock closes hydraulic shutoff valves, removing hydraulic power from and locking the flap drive brake. Conversely, any extension of the flaps restricts the wing sweep to less than 20° by means of the mechanical interlock.

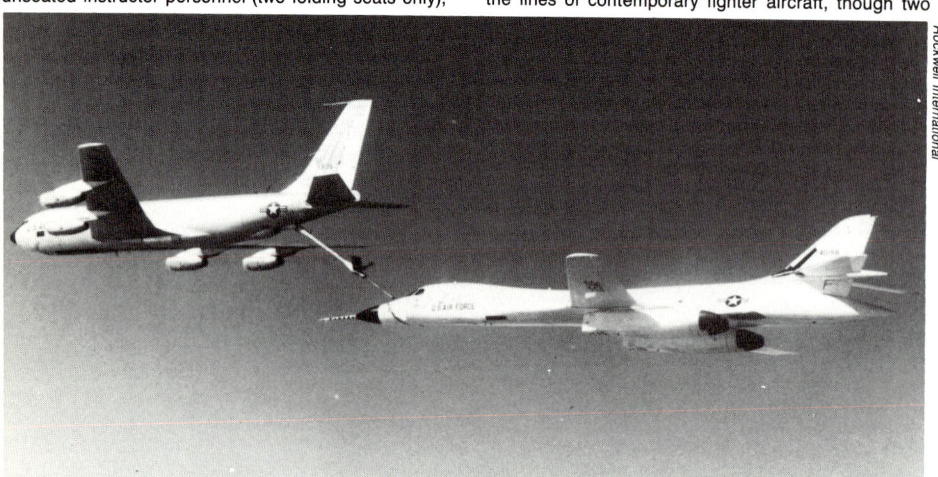

Inflight refueling was successfully accomplished for the first time using B-1A, 74-0158. Excellent control and throttle response give the B-1 high marks from both ''boomers'' and pilots. The inflight refueling receptacle is nose mounted, permitting the pilot an excellent view of boom connect and disconnect activity.

Roll control when the wings are swept is maintained via the aforementioned slab stabilators; with the wings extended, roll control is maintained via four-segment airbrake/spoilers on each outer wing, forward of the outer four flap segments. These airbrake/spoilers have a maximum upward deflection of 70°. All control surfaces are operated electro-hydraulically by rods, cables, pulleys, and bellcrank levers, except for the two outboard spoilers on each wing which are controlled by a fly-by-wire system.

The B-1B's all-steel landing gear is essentially the same as that of the B-1A, though it has been strengthened where necessary to accommodate the B-1B's higher gross take-off weights. Basically, the landing gear is of the tricycle type and is fully retractable into gear wells located in the nose and the wing root and center fuselage sections just inboard of the engine nacelles. Each main unit, which retracts inward and rearward, has two pairs of wheels in tandem. The steerable (75° left or right of center) nose unit has twin wheels and retracts forward. An oleo-pneumatic shock absorber is integral with each unit. The wheels are steel and the disc brakes are of state-of-the-art carbon design. The mainwheel diameter is 23.5'' and the tire size is 46 x 16-325. Tire specs include a 30-ply rating and a standard pressure of between 220 and 275 lbs. sq.'' The nosewheel diameter is 16'' and the tire size is 35 x 11.5-16. Tire specs include a 22-ply rating and a standard pressure of 210 lbs. sq.''

Miscellaneous systems include an air-conditioning and pressurization system; four 4,000 psi/63 gals. per min. independent hydraulic systems for actuation of wing sweep, control surfaces, landing gear and weapons bay doors; gas/oil reservoirs pressurized to approx. 160 lbs. sq.''; a main electrical system with three 105/115 kVA integrated engine driven constant-speed generators which supply 230/400V three-phase AC power at 400 Hz through four primary buses; a self-testing electrical multiplex system (EMUX) which utilizes several minicomputers and serves to control the B-1B's major subsystems by collecting and conditioning signals at remote terminals and transmitting them from point to point over a common data bus and at the same time supervising all signal data using a centralized controller/processor (requiring only two two-wire cables for its operations, the EMUX is designed to control such functions as electrical power distribution to subsystems and avionics equipment, engine instruments, environmental control system, fuel system, landing gear, lights, and weapons system operations; its use results in a considerable weight savings); APU's for providing self-start capability for operation from advance airfields and for driving an emergency generator to power the essential bus; a quadruplex automatic flight control system (AFCS) which is a split axis system providing a variety of pitch and roll, automatic guidance, and pilot assist modes of flight control operation as well as automatic throttle control; a flight director panel with heading hold, navigation, and automatic approach modes; a central air data computer; a gyro stabilization system; a structural mode control system (SMCS) which detects and automatically dampens structural bending mode oscillations in the vertical and lateral axes of the aircraft (bending oscillations are dampened through symmetrical or asymmetrical displacement of control vanes on each side of the forward fuselage with vertical damping being obtained through symmetrical displacement of the vanes and lateral bending being dampened through asymmetrical displacement—it functions only when the pitch and roll SCAS are in operation); and an engine fire extinguising system.

There are four major equipment bay areas including the forward equipment bay, the central equipment bay, the wheel well equipment bays (2), and the aft equipment bay. Additionally, there are two smaller bays just aft of the central bay, and two smaller bays called side fairing bays, one in each fuselage wing root. In addition, a bay has been incorporated into the horizontal stabilizer fairing to house the tail warning radar. There are two 15' long stores bays forward of the wing-carry-through structure and one 15' long stores bay aft of the main landing gear wells.

ARMAMENT AND ELECTRONICS:

The B-1B is an exceptionally complex weapon capable of carrying a wide variety of bombs, cruise missiles, and related ordnance. In order to get these devices near or over their target, it is equipped with a wide array of sophisticated electronic countermeasures gear, active countermeasures systems, state-of-the-art radar systems, highly advanced navigation systems, and numerous passive and active design and performance innovations.

Sporting dummy nose and tail cones and jury-rigged SMCS vanes, the prototype B-1B, 82-0001, is seen inside Rockwell's greatly expanded Palmdale facility shortly before being placed in the paint shop. Wearing a new low-visibility paint scheme, it was rolled-out for the first time on September 4, 1984.

Basically, the B-1B uses radar and navigation equipment technology developed for the latest U.S. fighter aircraft such as the General Dynamics F-16, and avionics technology from the Boeing B-52G/H updated offensive avionics system (OAS). Standard government furnished equipment includes communications, IFF, ILS, intercom, miscellaneous navigation equipment, the AN/APN-224 radar altimeter (similar to that equipping the B-52G/H), an altimeter indicator, and a transponder.

The offensive avionics system (OAS) which provides the functions of navigation and weapons delivery, stores management, defense/RFS/ECMS, and terrain following, includes a high-accuracy inertial navigation system (developed from that used in the F-16); an AN/APN-218 or -230 Doppler velocity sensor comprising a single antenna/receiver/transmitter unit; an AN/APQ-164 multimode offensive radar system (ORS) derived from the F-16C's AN/APG-68 and which includes a low-observable phased-array antenna to provide low altitude terrain following and precise navigational functions (the B-1A's were equipped with F-111 systems which had separate antennas for terrain following and ground mapping; the first AN/APQ-164 was rolled out on November 15, 1983); eight avionics control units (ACU's) which include four for the offensive/defensive avionics system, one for the RFS/ECMS, one for the Central Integrated Test System (CITS), and two for terrain following are based on those used in the B-52G/H a mass storage device (MSD) that uses program instructions for navigation, weapons delivery, bomb damage assessment and, defensive system computation; and offensive display sets comprising three multi-function displays (two at the OSO's station and one at the DSO's station), an electronics display unit, and a video recorder similar to that used in the B-52G/H; electronic CRT display units modified from those developed for the original B-1A to allow the DSO to analyze threat situations and assign appropriate countermeasures; and data transfer units (identical to those in the B-52G/H) to program the offensive avionics and gather and store mission and flight data.

The offensive radar set (ORS) is a Doppler ground mapping system with two primary functions: (1) to provide terrain following and terrain avoidance data to the pilot and co-pilot; and (2) to provide map presentations

ANTENNAS

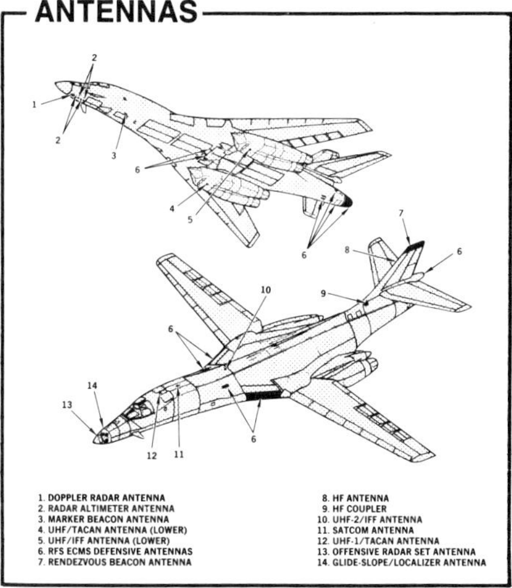

Vought Aero Products Division is one of several major subcontractors working with Rockwell International on the B-1B program. Vought produces the aft and after intermediate (shown) fuselage sections. A B-1B, possibly 83-0065, is visible in the background undergoing final assembly at the Palmdale facility.

The first B-1A, 74-0158, during the early stages of its flight test program at Edwards AFB. The aircraft then was undergoing systems maintenance inside the massive B-1 program hangar at Edwards. Noteworthy is the fact that the normally retracted capsule aerodynamic control vanes must be extended to permit bay access.

to the OSO for targeting, navigation, weather detection, and recognition of air and ground beacons; the ORS can also back up the Doppler velocity system by supplying velocity data to the navigation system. The ORS is controlled by the OSO through the Bomb/Nav panel, the OSO track handle, and the radar control panel. The radar map is displayed on the radar display unit (RDU).

The defensive avionics system utilizes the highly sophisticated and extraordinarily powerful AN/ALQ-161 system. Developed to support the original B-1A over a broad spectrum of missions, including deep solo penetration of hostile airspace, it has been extensively flight tested over a two-year period (being installed first in B-1A, 76-0174). A number of additions have extended both the frequency coverage and the repertoire of electronic jamming techniques of the original design. The current AN/ALQ-161 should be capable of accommodating the B-1B's needs until the mid-1990's.

The system consists of four major parts: (1) the AN/ALQ-161A radio frequency surveillance/electronics countermeasures system (RFS/ECMS); (2) the tail warning function (TWF); (3) the AN/ASQ-184 offensive avionics system defensive management system (DMS) and defensive controls and displays; and (4) the expendable countermeasures (EXCM) systems, and its 108 separate elements, of which more than one-third are antennas. Total cost per B-1B is expected to be around $20-million.

This aircraft system automatically monitors and displays received enemy radar data along the preplanned or selected flightpath, and assigns jamming and deception techniques to confuse or mislead enemy radar systems. Integral parts include the TWF which monitors the aft sector of the aircraft for possible threats and the EXCM system for dispensing infrared (IR) flares and chaff.

The AN/ALQ-161A system is highly modular with 108 integrated line replaceable units (LRU) distributed throughout the aircraft. This modularity, coupled with a standardized digital data communications network, allows the system to be easily updated to respond to future mission requirements. LRU's can be added or removed, and new LRU's incorporating new technology can easily be installed.

The AN/ALQ-161 is linked (via the data bus) to other equipment and to the DSO through the controls and displays of the AN/ASQ-184. It is capable of completely autonomous operation of the controls and displays if interface is lost.

The TWF is an automatic pulse doppler radar which detects airborne interceptors or missiles approaching from the rear of the aircraft. After detection and processing, the TWF discriminates between aircraft and missiles.

The TWF monitors the missile position and compares it to the prestored and enabled time-to-intercept and/or range-to-go data, and a missile warning tone is provided to the crew through the aircraft intercom. When a threat is detected and the signal is processed, a countermeasures command signal is dispatched and the associated azimuth and range information is displayed to the DSO. The DMS then selects the side of the aircraft from which expendable countermeasures should be dispensed, based on this data.

Aircraft and missile detections are presented on the threat situation format (TSF) display. Multiple missile threats are processed simultaneously, with the highest priority threats identified for DSO display.

The DMS provides the interface between the DSO and the defensive equipment. It uses part of the AN/ASQ-184 offensive avionics suite to give the DSO interface with the RFS/ECMS and the EXCM system. The AN/ASQ-184 components that interface with the defensive equipment are: the avionics control unit complex (ACUC) and software; the integrated keyboard (IKB) and multifunction display (MFD); the RFS/ECM control panel; the DSO power panel; the DSO track handle; and the electronic display unit (EDU) x 2.

The DSO uses these components for display of detected radar emitters and defensive order of battle (DOB) tables; for setting response priorities; for selection of countermeasures techniques; for threat avoidance; for assessment of techniques used; and for management of countermeasures resources. System interaction, displays, and responses are automatic, but controls are provided for manual intervention by the DSO.

Monitoring of the DMS is provided by displays and formats presented on two EDU's and one MFD. The two EDU's display the TSF and panoramic format (PF), while the MFD displays the logic tree options available in response to operator inputs through the IKB. When power is applied to the RFS/ECM system, the TSF display is initialized on the right EDU while the PF display is initialized on the left EDU.

The expendable countermeasures system (EXCM) is a software controlled, automatically or manually initiated, flare and chaff dispensing system. The EXCM consists of eight interchangeable flare or chaff dispensers located on top of the fuselage aft of the crew compartment, a controller, and DSO station controls and displays. Dispensing of chaff or flares is controlled by the DSO via the EXCM controller.

The aircraft has eight dispensing locations, organized in two banks of four each, identified as the left bank (dispensers 1, 3, 5, and 7) and the right bank (dispensers 2, 4, 6, and 8). Each dispenser location may be loaded with a dispenser which contains up to 12 flares or up to

120 chaff cartridges.

This network supported by the AN/ALQ-161 can control the jamming chains so rapidly that each can jam signals from many radars simultaneously. The numerous jamming chains are deployed around the periphery of the B-1B to jam signals in any frequency band coming from any direction. By means of this receiving subsystem new signals can be picked up, identified, and then jammed, with optimized jamming techniques, in a fraction of a second. One of the advantages of having the receiving function completely integrated with the jamming function, which was unique to the AN/ALQ-161 when it was first designed, is that it allows the receiving system to detect new signals and continue to monitor old signals while jamming in the same frequency band. A special subsystem allows this to be accomplished by monitoring the output of the jamming transmitters and adjusting the receivers continuously. All main systems computers on the B-1B, including the AN/ALQ-161's main computer, are identical, and communicate over a time multiplexing military standard data bus designated 1553.

It also uses this bus to send data to the central integrated test system (CITS) which records all inflight failures and battle damage for later diagnosis and repair. The CITS provides 95% fault detection and 75% fault isolation capability. Within the AN/ALQ-161 itself there is also a local status monitoring network called SEAT (status evaluation and test) which reports to CITS and allows the system automatically to route electronic signals around failed components and maintain full jamming response against the highest priority threat signals. Exclusive of cabling, displays, and controls, the current AN/ALQ-161 system weighs approximately 5,200 lbs. and consumes about 120 kW of power in a maximum power jamming mode.

The B-1B is equipped with three large internal weapons bays consisting of a two-bay section forward of the main gear retraction wells, and a single bay aft. The two bay-section is 31'3'' in length and the single-bay section is 15'0''. All three bays are each equipped with retractable spoilers at the forward end of each bay (to reduce acoustic loads on the doors) and two single-piece hydraulically actuated composite construction doors. The doors have variable opening capabilities dictated by the type of weapon being released. Non-nuclear gravity bombs are released with the doors fully open; air-launched cruise missiles and nuclear weapons are released with the doors only partially open.

On B-1B's 9 through 100, the forward double bay is equipped with a movable bulkhead (all earlier aircraft, with the exception of 82-0001, will be updated to incorporate this system as time permits) permitting the accommodation of a wide variety of weapons of various sizes and loads. The bulkhead can be repositioned to provide two 15' bays, one 22' bay plus an 8' bay forward, or left out entirely to provide one 31' bay. The B-1B's internal capacity in a nuclear role includes up to eight AGM-86B air-launched cruise missiles (ALCM), twenty-four AGM-69 short range attack missiles (SRAM), twelve B-28 or twenty-four B-61 or B-83 free-fall nuclear bombs. The aircraft also is equipped with eight external stores stations beneath the fuselage that can be used to accommodate an additional fourteen ALCM's.

In the non-nuclear role, the B-1B's capacity includes a maximum of up to eighty-four 500 lb. Mk.82 AIR high drag gravity bombs. The weapons bays can also be utilized for carrying auxiliary fuel tanks.

The B-1B's stores management system (SMS) is controlled by the weapons delivery ACU (WDACU). The SMS provides for the automatic or manually initiated release

Very late in its career, and after its removal from the actual B-1A flight test program, B-1A, 74-0158, is seen painted in the low-visibility camouflage scheme created primarily for use on the B-1B. This photo, taken at Edwards AFB during March, 1985, reveals the missing vertical fin cap, the highly tapered tail cone, the extremely conical nose radome, and the nose test boom that were all distinctive features of this first aircraft.

of nuclear or non-nuclear weapons in the desired mode as well as jettison release. Its primary function is to prepare missiles and bombs for release, maintain these weapons in a ready condition, and release them at the selected target. The SMS also provides methods to jettison the stores, modify the preloaded mission program, and support training missions. The training may be done with software simulation of the weapons, or with dummy weapons and/or instrumented flight missiles.

The system also has the capability of releasing functional missiles beyond the range of target defenses. The missiles can be retargeted any time before missile launch. After missile power is applied, warmup and inflight alignment of the missile inertial reference unit requires only a brief period during the flight. After fine alignment of the missile has been accomplished, it is ready for launch. The system is capable of navigation and release of weapons automatically; manual release commanded by the OSO is also possible.

Rotary launchers are provided for the carriage and release of nuclear weapons. There are three different types of rotary launchers currently available for use in the B-1B: (1) gravity weapon launcher; (2) SRAM launcher; and (3) the Common Strategic Rotary Launcher (CSRL)—used for the ALCM or gravity weapons and installed only in the intermediate weapons bay. The launchers are loaded with weapons before installation.

A non-nuclear weapons suspension and release system may be installed in any of the three weapons bays. This unit is used for individual release of non-nuclear weapons. It is installed using the same attach points as the nuclear rotary launchers.

The following is a listing, assembled by contributing researcher Craig Kaston, that describes the various configuration differences noted between the various B-1A's and the new B-1B's; this list is based on observed and reported external configuration changes and as such, probably is not complete:

LOCATION	-1A or -1B	A/C #	NOTES
Radome	-1A	1,2,3	long, double cone radome
	-1A	1,2	long test boom
	-1A	3	short pitot boom
	-1A	4	short radome now replaced by B-1B radome; also has short pitot boom
	-1B	all	short ogival radome
	-1B	1	short pitot boom; subsequent a/c have none
Fuselage forward of cockpit	-1A	1,2,3	short, 1 access door, 1 pitot per side
	-1A	4	long, at least 2 access doors, 2 pitot tubes further forward
	-1B	all	same as B-1A#4
SMCS vane position	-1A	1,2,3	vane leading edge in line with leading edge of nose landing gear door
	-1A	4	moved approx. 1' forward
	-1B	all	same as B-1A#4
Cockpit area	-1A	1,2,3	escape module; riser cover between eye-brow windows; module fins partially cover mid-fuselage avionics bay access doors; diagonal side cockpit window post; module rocket visible through nose gear well
	-1A	4	ejection seats; no module, riser cover, fins, rocket motor; vertical side cockpit window post; removable panels above ejection seats
	1B	all	same as B-1A#4 except windows added for DSO and OSO stations
Nose landing gear	-1A	1,2,3	two-piece beam with massive drag link
	-1A	4	dual "V" type drag link
	-1B	all	same as B-1A#4
Forward mid-fuselage	-1A	1,2,3	three large external avionics bay access doors per a/c side
	-1A	4	doors omitted due to internal access
	-1B	all	same as B-1A#4 with addition of two large angled antennas
Wing glove leading edge	-1A	1,2,3	metal
	-1A	4	poly-quartz fairing
	-1B	all	same as B-1A#4
Bottom mid-fuselage	-1A	1,2	no sensors
Engine nacelle inlet	-1A	1,2,3,4	2-dimensional external compression inlet
	-1B	all	fixed-geometry inlet incorporating low RCS baffling
Engine nacelle	-1A	1,2,3	solid keel between nacelles
Exhaust nozzles	-1A	1,2,3,4	pre-production engines; long nozzles
	-1B	all	production engines; short nozzles
Wing cover	-1A	1,2,3	single panel; rides on top of wing as wing swings back
	-1A	4	same as 1,2,3, except wing intrusion box eliminated
	-1B	all	wing has canvas-flap-type side entry into fuselage fairing
Aft fuselage	-1A	1,2,3	pointed tailcone
	-1A	1	flow pod mod from 3/77 to 5/77
	-1A	1,2,3	vortex generators
	-1A	4	blunt tailcone/tail radome; cut-outs for aft facing sensor antennas; forward looking camera noted on vertical stabilizer fin cap 9/82
	-1B	all	same as B-1A#4 except for internal equipment
Horizontal/vertical stabilizer junction	-1A	1,2,3	pointed aft facing fairing
	-1A	4	blunt aft facing fairing
	-1B	all	same as B-1A#4

B-1A test aircraft modification notes:

#1 (74-0158) flow pod modification, 3/77; demodified; aft fuselage vortex generators added; vanes for flutter test added; painted green/gray during 1984 after flight test program was completed

#2 (74-0159) structural test airframe; aft fuselage vortex generators added; used with no offensive or defensive avionics for weapon separation tests; B-1B test markings added; internal modifications for B-1B test; painted green/gray; updated to B-1B flight control system configuration, used for continued engine and aircraft systems testing and for continued weapons separation tests

#3 (74-0160) limited avionics test aircraft; aft fuselage vortex generators added; fuselage "spine" TWT/waveguide added; painted in desert colors; "Crosseye" electronic countermeasures system added; waveguides and fairings added on forward fuselage; waveguides added beneath wings; navigation lights removed from wingtips; antennas added; "Crosseye" ECM package partially removed

#4 (76-0174) ECM/ESM/ECCM test aircraft; fuselage "spine" TWT/waveguide added; painted in desert colors; skin patch installed after aft left escape hatch was lost in flight at Andrews AFB during return flight from Farnborough Airshow; new hatch fabricated and installed; fuselage "spine" removed; new radar system and avionics complement installed; B-1B-type radome and antennas added; painted in green/gray colors

B-1B test aircraft modification notes:

#1 (82-0001) highly instrumented, full configuration aircraft to test B-1B systems, and is presently not scheduled for delivery to SAC

#2 (83-0065) used for flight manual and maintenance manual validation and verification prior to its delivery to Dyess AFB

#9 (84-0049) scheduled for delivery during March, 1986; first aircraft w/movable bulkhead feature between the forward and intermediate weapons bays; it will be used for advanced weapon testing, including the AGM-86B ALCM

POWERPLANT:

Both the B-1A and B-1B are powered by General Electric F101 augmented turbofan engines. The following is a chronological listing of F101 milestones and associated dates:

Contract Award by U.S. Air Force	June 1970
First Engine to Test	April 1972
Preliminary Flight Rating Test Approved by U.S. Air Force	March 1974
First Flight of B-1	December 1974
Product Verification Completed	August 1976
Continued Engineering Development (CED) Commenced	August 1976
B-1 Production Decision	November 1976
F101-GE-100 Production Contract Received	November 1976
B-1 Production Cancellation	June 1977
Continuing Engineering Development (CED) Complete	March 1981
B-1 Flight Test Program Completed	April 1981
Presidential Recommendation for 100 B-1Bs	October 1981
Start F101-GE-102 Full Scale Development (FSD) ($128,000,000)	October 1981
FSD Contract Award	February 1982
F101-GE-102 Production Contract Received ($125,000,000)	April 1982
Completion of FSD	September 1983
First Production Engine Shipped	September 1983
Flight Test Completion	June 1986

The early B-1A's were specifically powered by YF101-GE-100 pre-production samples (the first XF101 was delivered to Rockwell on June 14, 1973, to use for powerplant nacelle tests), and the B-1B's are powered by the F-101-GE-102 engine. The F101 core components are common with both the GE F101 Derivative Fighter Engine (DFE) military engine, and the CFM-56 civil engine. By May, 1981, F101 engines had logged 347 flights and 7,600 engine flight hours on the B-1. The F101-GE-102 major gas generator components had accumulated, by September, 1982, over 65,000 hours of F101, F101 DFE, and CFM 56 factory, flight test, and in-service experience. In accelerated mission testing (which simulates actual engine operation in the B-1B), the F101-GE-102 demonstrated a 3,000 hour hot section life and a 10,000 hour cold section life. The F101-GE-102 is rated at 30,750 lbs. thrust in full afterburner.

Following the rebirth of the B-1 under the B-1B program, General Electric, with a $182,000,000 full-scale development contract from the Air Force in hand, took three F101-GE-102 engines and placed them in a test program exploring performance, endurance, and structural integrity parameters. After 190 engine test hours, the performance engine demonstrated that it was equal to or better than what was called for in the USAF contract specifications. The first series of tests was completed by GE at the end of 1982. A second performance test phase, which included 150 hours of altitude testing at the Arnold Engineering Development Center in Tullahoma, Tennessee, began during May, 1983, and continued through July—with higher than expected results.

A second engine completed 380 hours of endurance testing under the accelerated mission testing program at the end of March, 1983. Following engine parts inspection by the U.S. Government and General Electric, the engine was reassembled to begin an additional 350 hours of testing at GE's Evendale, Ohio, facility. This phase was completed during the fall of 1983.

The F101-GE-102 was a dual-rotor design with a bypass ratio of close to 2. It incorporates a simplified exhaust nozzle to reduce weight and neutral position bleed air extraction slots to permit built-up engine assemblies to be installed in any engine position.

The fan has inlet guide vanes with variable trailing flaps. The two fan stages have solid titanium blades with tip shrouds. Inlet guide vanes and fan vanes are installed in a horizontally split casing which permits blades and vanes to be individually replaceable. The fan has a pressure ratio of over 2 and the airflow rate is approximately 350 lbs. per sec.

The compressor section consists of nine stages, with a pressure ratio of over 11. The first three vane stages and inlet guide vanes are variable. The casing is split horizontally and the forward section is of titanium and the aft section of steel. Inertia welded discs make a continuous steel drum. Blades and vanes are individually replaceable.

The combustor is of the very short annular type with dual cone nozzles to inject fuel into the dome area.

The high pressure turbine is a single-stage, high energy extraction design. The blades and vanes are hollow airfoils which are convective and film cooled. The stationary shroud is segmented and cooled to provide tip clearance control.

The low pressure turbine consists of two stages and is tip-shrouded and uncooled. The blades are individually replaceable and second stage blades are replaceable in segmented groups.

The augmentor, or afterburner, is of the mixed flow type, with a convoluted flow mixer to provide efficient mixing and burning of both fan and core streams. Fan and core flows are mixed in the plane of the flameholder where ignition is started at the inner ring. The radial flame holders are located in the engine core stream, this improving lightoff and stable high altitude operation.

The exhaust nozzle is of the convergent-divergent type. Area variations are obtained by hydraulic actuators which move an actuation ring which positions the segmented flaps and seals through a series of cams and links.

The F101-GE-102 is 181'' in length, has a diameter of 55'', and has a dry weight of 4,400 lbs. It is virtually smokeless.

The engines are mounted in podded pairs under each wing fixed root section, near the aircraft c.g., this giving improved stability during low-altitude high-turbulence conditions.

B-1A nacelles were originally designed to accommodate the aircraft's Mach 2 performance requirement, which thus dictated that the intakes be of the variable geometry type. With the demise of the high-altitude supersonic mission requirement and a decision to produce the reconfigured B-1B, a revised nacelle configuration was created, this providing the aircraft with only a marginally supersonic speed capability, but concommitantly greatly reducing the B-1B's RCS. The latter was accomplished by installing baffling plates in the intake throat, this very effectively lowering the return energy created by the spinning compressor turbine.

The B-1B is equipped with eight sizable internal fuel tanks with six located in the fuselage and one in each wing. The integral tanks are the forward tank, the forward intermediate tank, the aft intermediate tank, the aft tank, two main tanks (in the wing-carry-through structure), and the wing outer panel tanks. There is also provision for auxiliary fuel tanks to be carried in the two forward weapons bays and beneath the fuselage. The fuel management panel is located in the cockpit just to the right of the centerline of the forward instrument panel. All of the necessary controls for manual as well as automatic operation of the fuel supply system are on the panel. This panel also contains the individual fuel quantity displays for all fuel storage in the aircraft. The B-1B provides a considerable increase in fuel capacity over that of the B-1A. An inflight refueling receptacle is mounted in the upper nose section, just forward of the windscreen.

FUEL TANK QUANTITIES

TANK	FUEL QUANTITY POUNDS (GALLONS) *JP-4(MIL-T-5624)	TOTAL FUEL AVAILABLE PER TANK
FORWARD (NO. 1)	32,207 (4,954.9)	31,206 (4,800.9)
FORWARD INTERMEDIATE (NO. 2)	38,929 (5,989.1)	37,951 (5,838.6)
AFT INTERMEDIATE (NO. 3)	24,029 (3,696.8)	23,813 (3,663.5)
AFT (NO. 4)	52,815 (8,125.4)	51,915 (7,986.9)
MAIN	21,010 (3,232.3)	20,524 (3,157.5)
WG (L.R.) (WING)	33,264 (5,117.5)	30,141 (4,637.1)
TOTAL FUEL QUANTITY	202,254 (31,116.0)	195,550 (30,084.5)
ST BAY 180 INCHES	19,842 (31,116.0)	19,340 (2,975.4)
91 INCHES	8,782 (1,351.1)	8,475 (1,303.8)

Based on Test Data—Estimated:
*Weights (volume) given is for JP-4 at Standard Day Temperature for a density of 6.5 pounds per gallon.

SPECIFICATIONS AND PERFORMANCE:

	B-1A	B-1B
Fuselage length	150'2½'' (w/nose boom)	147'0''
Wingspan (unswept)	136'8½''	136'8½''
Wingspan (swept)	78'2½''	78'2½''
Wing area (gross)	1,950 sq.'	1,950 sq.'
Wing loading	200 lbs. sq.'	244.6 lbs. sq.'
Horizontal stabilator span	44'10''	44'10''
Height	33'7¼''	33'7¼''
Wheel track (to c/1 of shock struts)	14'6''	14'6''
Wheelbase	57'6''	57'6''
Empty weight	140,000 lbs.	192,000 lbs.
Gross ramp weight	395,000 lbs.	485,00 lbs.
Gross takeoof weight	389,800 lbs.	477,000 lbs.
Max. landing weight	350,000 lbs.	360,000 lbs.
Max. speed @ 50,000'	Mach 2.0 1,320 mph	Mach 1.25 792mph
Cruising speed @ 500'	Mach .85	Mach .92
Combat ceiling	approx. 62,000'	approx. 60,000'
Max. unrefueled range	5,300 n. miles 6,100 miles	6,475 n. miles 7,455 miles

PRODUCTION AND SERIAL NUMBER

B-1A

PRODUCTION NUMBER	SERIAL NO.	PRODUCTION NUMBER	SERIAL NO.	PRODUCTION NUMBER	SERIAL NO.
1.	74-0158	2.	74-0159	3.	74-0160
4.	76-0174				

B-1B

PRODUCTION NUMBER	SERIAL NO.	PRODUCTION NUMBER	SERIAL NO.	PRODUCTION NUMBER	SERIAL NO.
1.	82-0001	35.	85-0075	68.	86-0108
2.	83-0065	36.	85-0076	69.	86-0109
3.	83-0066	37.	85-0077	70.	86-0110
4.	83-0067	38.	85-0078	71.	86-0111
5.	83-0068	39.	85-0079	72.	86-0112
6.	83-0069	40.	85-0080	73.	86-0113
7.	83-0070	41.	85-0081	74.	86-0114
8.	83-0071	42.	85-0082	75.	86-0115
9.	84-0049	43.	85-0083	76.	86-0116
10.	84-0050	44.	85-0084	77.	86-0117
11.	84-0051	45.	85-0085	78.	86-0118
12.	84-0052	46.	85-0086	79.	86-0119
13.	84-0053	47.	85-0087	80.	86-0120
14.	84-0054	48.	85-0088	81.	86-0121
15.	84-0055	49.	85-0089	82.	86-0122
16.	84-0056	50.	85-0090	83.	86-0123
17.	84-0057	51.	85-0091	84.	86-0124
18.	84-0058	52.	85-0092	85.	86-0125
19.	85-0059	53.	86-0093	86.	86-0126
20.	85-0060	54.	86-0094	87.	86-0127
21.	85-0061	55.	86-0095	88.	86-0128
22.	85-0062	56.	86-0096	89.	86-0129
23.	85-0063	57.	86-0097	90.	86-0130
24.	85-0064	58.	86-0098	91.	86-0131
25.	85-0065	59.	86-0099	92.	86-0132
26.	85-0066	60.	86-0100	93.	86-0133
27.	85-0067	61.	86-0101	94.	86-0134
28.	85-0068	62.	86-0102	95.	86-0135
29.	85-0069	63.	86-0103	96.	86-0136
30.	85-0070	64.	86-0104	97.	86-0137
31.	85-0071	65.	86-0105	98.	86-0138
32.	85-0072	66.	86-0106	99.	86-0139
33.	85-0073	67.	86-0107	100.	86-0140
34.	85-0074				

AVAILABLE SCALE MODELS AND DECALS:

Kits

B-1A:
Airfix: 1/144th
Entex: 1/144th
Monogram: 1/110th

B-1B:
Minicraft: 1/144th
Monogram: 1/144th Snap-tite
Monogram: 1/72nd
Revell: 1/48th

Decals

No decal sheets have been released as of the date of this publication.

The B-1B's inflight refueling receptacle is mounted in the nose, just ahead of the windscreen. A hinged, flat panel covers the receptacle when it is not in use, this retracting when refueling is undertaken. White markings, which will soon go to a low visibility scheme, facilitate night refueling requirements.

The following is a detailed account of the various paint schemes worn by the various B-1A's and extant B-1B's as of the date of this publication:

B-1A PAINT SCHEMES

B-1A-1 (74-0158)

- **Delivery/Roll Out.** White with Rockwell International emblem in blue on tail, SAC band and shield on the nose.

- **B-1A Flight Test.** White - Rockwell International emblem removed.

- **B-1B Flight Test.** Aircraft painted B-1B camouflage:
    FS 36081 (Gray)
    FS 36118 (Gray)
    FS 34086 (Dark Green)
  Used for night air refueling visibility tests (ground test only, not flown during B-1B Flight Test Program).

B-1A-2 (74-0159)

- **Delivery/Roll Out.** White with SAC band and shield on the nose.

- **B-1A Flight Test.** Same as roll out with the number ''2'' added to both forward nose gear doors.

- **B-1B Flight Test.**
  (1) Initially white (B-1A test scheme) with red, white, and blue tail with the words "B-1B TEST PROGRAM" above the serial number on the tail.
  (2) B-1B camouflage:
     FS 36081 (Gray)
     FS 36118 (Gray)
     FS 34086 (Dark Green)
     with "U.S. AIR FORCE" in black on the forward fuselage side and black "USAF" on bottom of left wing and top of right wing.
  (3) Markings removed, only national insignia on side of rear fuselage and serial number on the tail. These are the markings that were on the aircraft when it crashed.

B-1A-3 (74-0160)

- **Delivery/Roll Out.** White with SAC band and shield on the nose.

- **B-1A Flight Test.**
  (1) Same as rollout with the number "3" added to both forward nose gear doors, and photo recognition circles (black circle with black and white alternating quarters) on the forward outboard side of each nacelle.
  (2) During ECM testing spine fairing was added to top of fuselage and aircraft was painted:
     FS 30140 (Brown)
     FS 20400 (Tan)
     FS 34079 (Green)
     FS 36622 (Light Gray)
     Light Gray underside. Desert camouflage.

5 **B-1B Flight Test.** Same desert camouflage as it has at the end of B-1A Flight Test. Used as media tour aircraft.

B-1A-4 (76-0174)

- **Delivery/Roll Out.** White with SAC band and shield on the nose.

- **B-1A Flight Test.**
  (1) Desert camouflage same as B-1A #3 with spine fairing on top of fuselage.
  (2) Radome, originally black, camouflage painted for flight to Farnborough air show (September 1982).

- **B-1B Flight Test.**
  (1) Desert camouflage, black B-1B radome added.
  (2) The spine fairing was removed and the aircraft was painted in the B-1B camouflage:
     FS 36081 (Gray)
     FS 36118 (Gray)
     FS 34086 (Dark Green)
  (3) B-1B camouflage with white air refueling marks.

B-1B #1 (82-0001)

- **Delivery/Roll Out.** B-1B camouflage:
     FS 36081 (Gray)
     FS 36118 (Gray)
     FS 34086 (Dark Green)
  Gold number "1" on right side of fuselage under cockpit window overlaid with SAC shield.

- **B-1B Test Program.**
  (1) Number "1" and SAC shield removed.
  (2) White air refueling marks added.
- **Delivery Flight to Dyess AFB.** SAC shield on left side of fuselage under windshield, 96th Bomb Wing emblem on right side of fuselage under windshield, and on the right fuselage side between the co-pilot's window and the OSO's window, a yellow five-pointed star containing the ABILENE/DYESS AFB B-1B emblem with the words "THE STAR OF ABILENE" in light blue.

B-1B #2 (83-0065)

- **Delivery to Edwards AFB.** B-1B camouflage with white air refueling marks.
- **Delivery to Dyess AFB.** Marked the same as B-1B #1 (82-0001) when delivered to Dyess.

B-1B (83-0065 - 83-0068) Aircraft at Dyess AFB
     FS 36081 (Gray)
     FS 36118 (Gray)
     FS 34086 (Dark Green)
  No special markings.

The B-1B's advanced AN/APQ-164 offensive radar system was tested by Westinghouse aboard this specially equipped and modified BAC One-Eleven (N-164W). The cabin section of the company-owned aircraft was converted to accept test consoles and actual B-1B OSO displays. Test flights began during July, 1984.

Lockheed C-141A, 61-2777 (the third C-141A built), also was modified for use as a B-1 systems testbed. This aircraft was equipped with defensive systems avionics and related hardware in its fuselage and in its specially modified tail and an additional fairing on the left side of the forward fuselage.

The B-1's defensive system, referred to as the AN/ALQ-161, was developed by AIL/Eaton. The test program utilizing C-141A, 61-2777, permitted exploration of the system's numerous capabilities while identifying problems and anomalies before installation in production B-1B aircraft.

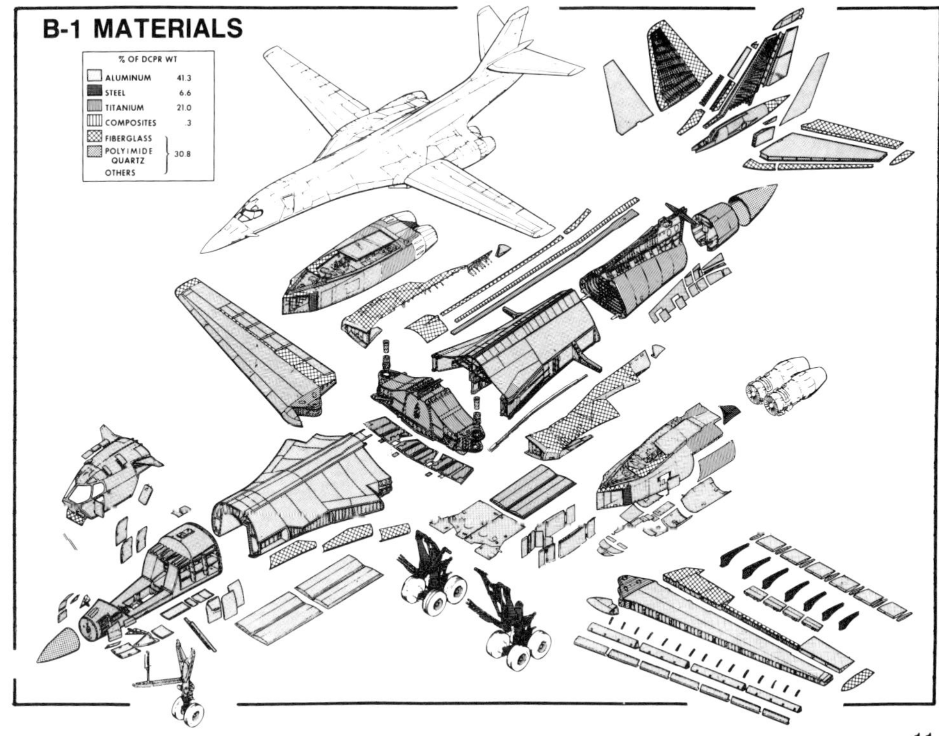

B-1A flight test operations were conducted from Edwards AFB utilizing a hangar capable of accommodating up to four B-1's at any one time. B-1A's, 74-0160 (left), and 74-0158, are seen inside the Edwards hangar undergoing pre-flight maintenance during their flight test program in 1975.

Two inflight views of B-1A, 74-0159, during the course of its flight test program at Edwards. The view on the left shows the aircraft with its wings fully swept to 67° 30-min.; the view on the right shows the wings at the minimum sweep angle of 15°. The wing sweep angle is infinitely variable.

B-1A, 74-0159, is seen during maintenance at Edwards. Notable is the tufting discernible on the aircraft tail. Visual identification of airflow anomalies in this area eventually led to the addition of vortex generators on all production aircraft.

The second B-1A, 74-0159, was modified in early 1983 to accommodate various B-1B subsystems. Following completion of this modification, it was given a distinctive paint scheme on its vertical fin and rudder.

B-1A, 74-0159, is seen with wings in their fully swept position. Visible also are the various camera installations added to monitor the weapons release tests. The wing root knuckle fairing is also readily discernible.

B-1A, 74-0159, is seen during acceleration tests over Edwards AFB. All four General Electric F101 engines are operating in full afterburner, and the wings are at maximum sweep. The B-1A was capable of speeds in excess of Mach 2.

B-1A, 74-0159, was painted in the B-1B camouflage scheme shortly after the B-1B systems test program got underway at Edwards. This pattern was eventually applied to three of the four B-1A's.

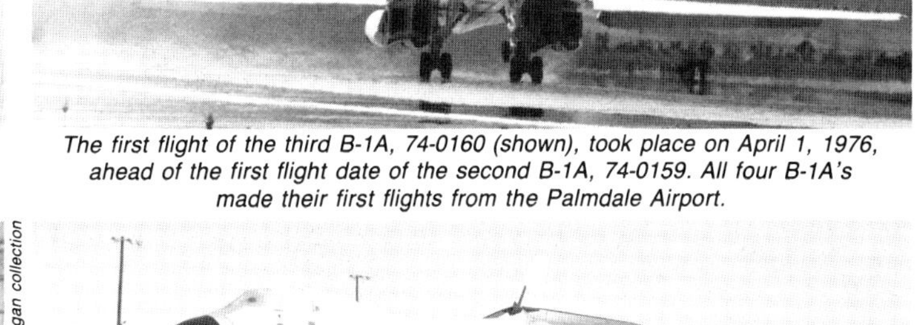

The first flight of the third B-1A, 74-0160 (shown), took place on April 1, 1976, ahead of the first flight date of the second B-1A, 74-0159. All four B-1A's made their first flights from the Palmdale Airport.

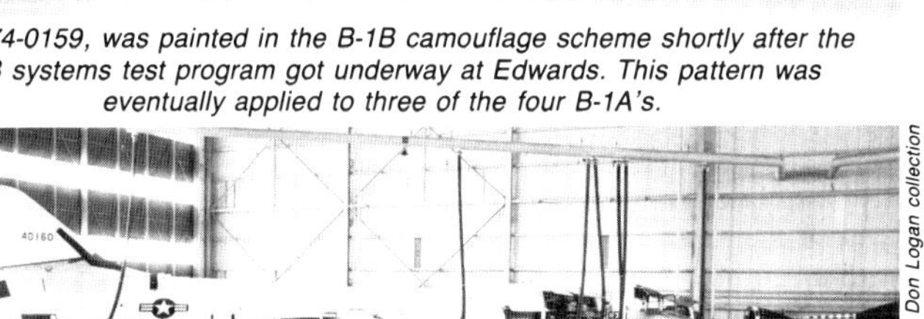

Large umbilicals seen hanging from the ceiling of the main Edwards AFB B-1 hangar over B-1A, 74-0160, are flexible air-conditioning ducts which deliver cool air to avionics and other temperature-sensitive components.

Following roll-out on November 7, 1975, B-1A, 74-0160, is seen being backed into position on the run-up ramp at Palmdale, just outside the main Rockwell facility there. The extended wing spoilers are noteworthy.

B-1A, 74-0160, is seen being moved into position for static display during an annual Edwards AFB open house. At the time, the aircraft was marked for ground tracking while undertaking weapons release tests. Note the black wheels.

While being utilized to test the B-1's offensive and defensive avionics system, B-1A, 74-0160, was modified to incorporate a large wave guide in the form of a dorsal spine, and was repainted in desert camouflage.

B-1A, 74-0160, logged the longest B-1A flight. This consisted of a round-trip mission between Edwards AFB, California, and Eglin AFB, Florida. It took more than 11 hours; of which 4 hours were spent on the Eglin AFB test range.

The B-1 is optimized for low altitude penetration of enemy airspace. B-1A, 74-0160, is seen during one of many low altitude sorties around Edwards AFB. Low altitude runs, due to thermal activity, tend to be fatiguing for the crew.

Rear view of B-1A, 74-0160, while undergoing maintenance at Edwards AFB. Air conditioning ducting is an integral part of virtually all B-1 ground operations and is usually accommodated by mobile air conditioning ground carts.

Another view of B-1A, 74-0160, at the beginning of its first flight which took place from Rockwell's Palmdale facility on April 1, 1976. After a flight of 4 hrs. and 54 min., it landed without incident at Edwards AFB, there joining B-1A, 74-0158.

Don Logan collection

The last B-1A to be built was 76-0174. It took to the air for the first time almost three years after its predecessors. This photo shows 76-0174 in its original all-white paint scheme. It was camouflaged shortly after entering flight test.

Don Logan collection

B-1A, 76-0174, was built as a testbed for what were essentially operational offensive and defensive avionics systems. As shown, it was equipped with the ''Crosseye'' ECM package and its associated dorsal spine modification.

Craig Kaston

Under contract to the Air Force, Rockwell modified B-1A, 76-0174, in order to bring it up to B-1B standards. Included were operationally configured offensive and defensive avionics systems, and a B-1B-type camouflage scheme.

Don Logan

With the exception of its intakes, wing/fuselage fairings, and missing DSO/OSO station observation windows, B-1A, 76-0174, is virtually indistinguishable from production B-1B's.

David Morgan

The first B-1B to arrive at Dyess AFB was the prototype aircraft, 82-0001. Painted to accommodate the arrival ceremonies scheduled originally for 83-0065 it was returned to Edwards AFB after the latter's arrival at Dyess.

Rockwell International

Following completion, B-1B, 82-0001, is seen inside a specially designed acoustical attenuation facility at Rockwell's Palmdale plant. The walls are designed to mute engine sounds during propulsion system ground testing.

Craig Kaston

Another view of B-1B, 82-0001, showing it at Edwards while hooked up to its full complement of air conditioning ducting. B-1B, 84-0049, the ninth B-1B, is expected also to be utilized as a flight test aircraft at Edwards AFB.

Don Logan collection

B-1B, 82-0001, in low-speed flight over Edwards. Visible are the extended leading edge slats, the extended Fowler-type flaps, and the landing gear. High-lift devices and variable-sweep wings make the B-1B fairly docile at low speed.

A line up at Dyess AFB, Texas, of three of the first four operational B-1B's. From left to right are aircraft 83-0068, 83-0067, and 83-0066. A fifth aircraft will have arrived by the end of March, 1986. Upgrading of Dyess AFB facilities has been extensive. Several new hangars capable of accommodating several B-1B's at one time are scheduled for completion by the end of 1986, and a vastly improved weapons storage bunker will be fully operational by the middle of the year.

B-1B, 83-0065, upon landing at Offutt AFB, Nebraska, during its delivery flight to Dyess AFB, was originally scheduled to be the first operational B-1B. A propulsion system anomaly delayed arrival at Dyess for several days.

Close-up of B-1B, 82-0001, showing the special markings painted on its right side in commemoration of the delivery of the first operational B-1B to Dyess AFB. These same markings were later applied to 83-0065.

Following repair, B-1B, 83-0065, was flown from Offutt AFB to Dyess AFB, and there officially handed over to SAC. Air-conditioning ducting is particularly prominent in this view taken at Dyess shortly after 83-0065's arrival.

Between training flights at Dyess AFB, B-1B, 83-0065, is presently serving as a ground maintenance trainer for B-1B support personnel. Dyess AFB's B-1B experience will set criteria for other B-1B Wings as they are activated.

Visible on the fuselage side just behind the windscreen is "The Star of Abilene" logo painted on B-1B, 83-0065, only. Maintenance and miscellaneous mechanical anomalies have seriously affected the flight scheduling of the B-1B.

Rear view of B-1B, 83-0065, provides good detail of the empennage's circular cross section, the required vortex generators, and the raised overwing glove fairings that accommodate wing sweep requirements.

The second B-1B to be delivered to Dyess was 83-0066 (left). This view, along with the nose section view of B-1A, 74-0160, permits an interesting comparison between the prototype and the production aircraft. Many of the changes, such as the location of the SMCS vanes, are subtle, but others, such as the redesign of the nose landing gear retraction strut, are quite distinctive. Other changes include a revised windscreen post and a more conical nose radome.

B-1B, 83-0066, on the ramp at Dyess AFB. All B-1B's have virtually invisible markings. Low visibility, in the form of radar absorbent paint and a matte finish, is just one of the many factors contributing to the B-1B's stealth characteristics.

B-1B, 83-0067, was the third B-1B to be assigned to Dyess AFB, arriving in early February, 1986. In this view, the open nose radome and exposed oval Westinghouse AN/APQ-164 radar antenna are noteworthy.

The fourth B-1B to arrive at Dyess AFB was 83-0068. This aircraft is virtually identical to its stablemates, differing only in its serial number. Note that the wing leading edge, underneath the wing slats, is painted white.

As can be seen in this view of 83-0068, in order to facilitate identification by ground personnel, the last four digits of the aircraft serial number are now painted on the insides of the nose gear well doors.

The B-1B, because of the sensitive nature of its intake radar attenuation baffling, is almost always seen with its intake covers in place and bags over its exhaust nozzles. This direct front view of B-1B, 83-0068, illustrates the spaghetti-like tangle created by the flexible air-conditioning ducting. No less than four duct attachment points are provided, these serving to cool various avionics and miscellaneous subsystem compartments.

Dennis Jenkins

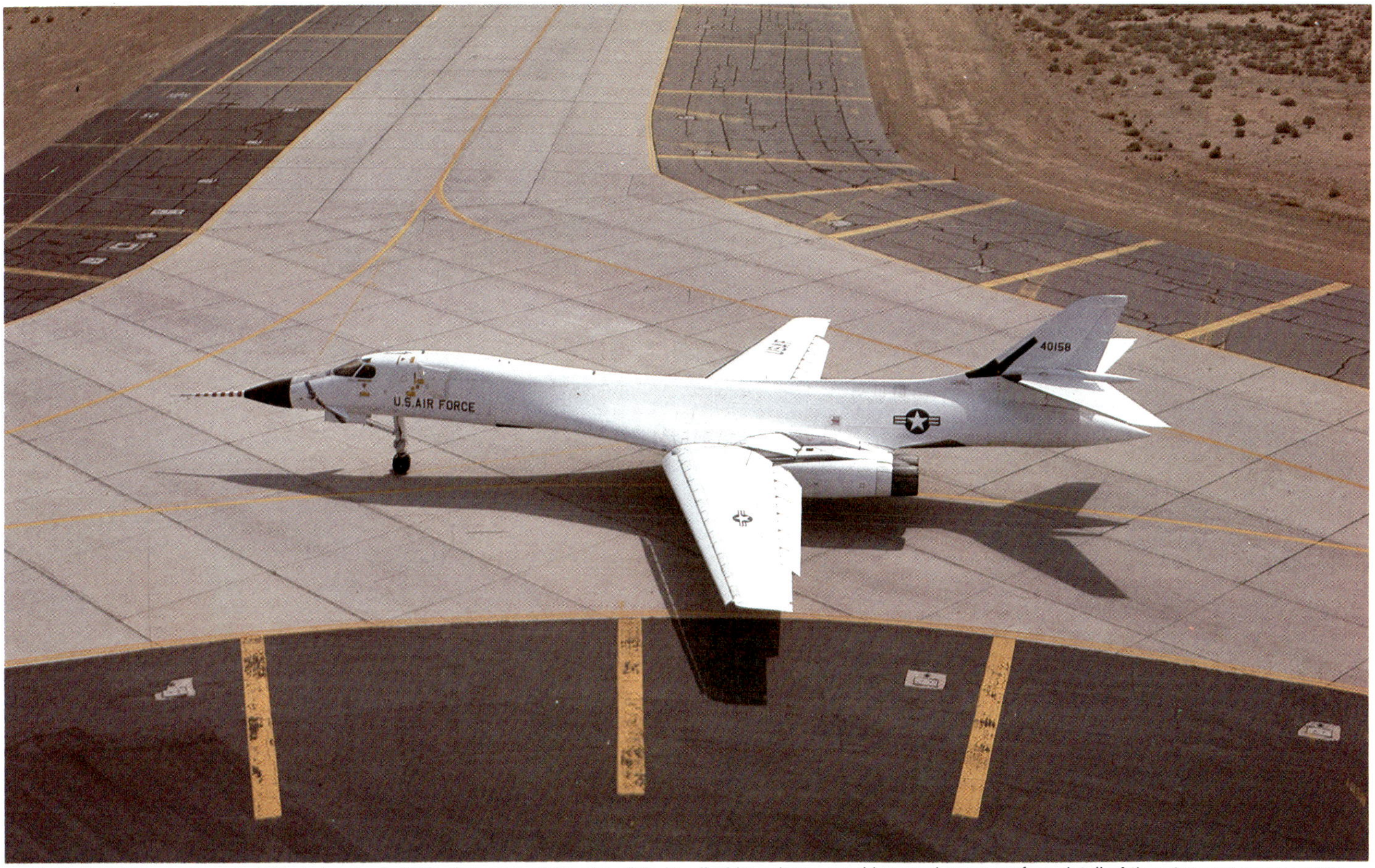

B-1A, 74-0158, at Edwards AFB during April, 1978. This view of the aircraft in its all-white scheme provides good upper surface detail of the wing root section glove fairing and the wing leading and trailing edge slats and flaps, respectively. The all-white paint scheme was particularly suitable for the Edwards AFB environment where daytime temperatures during the summer could easily exceed 100°. All four B-1A's were originally flown in all-white paint.

Craig Kaston

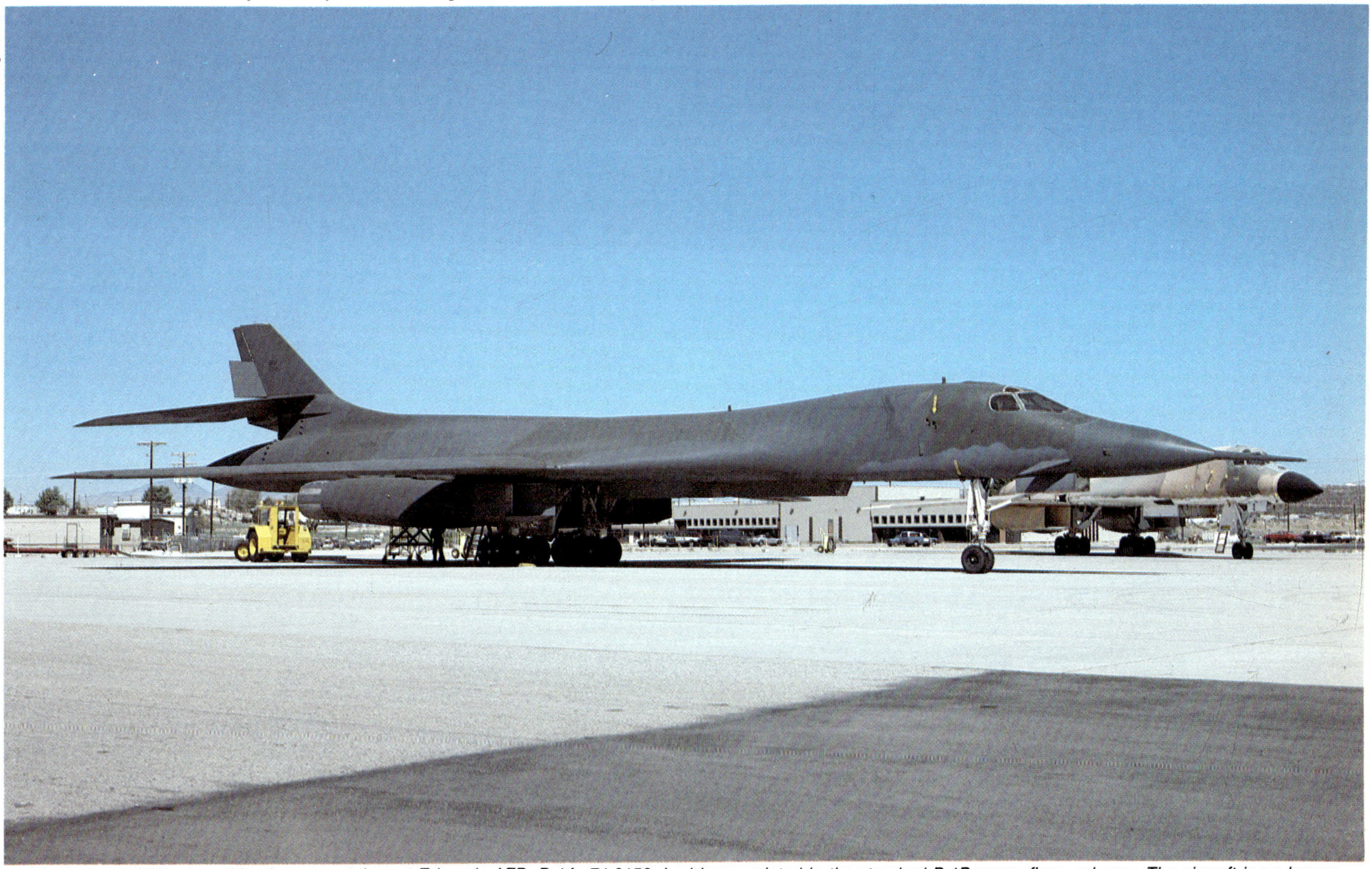

By August, 1985, when this photo was taken at Edwards AFB, B-1A, 74-0158, had been painted in the standard B-1B camouflage scheme. The aircraft is no longer participating in the B-1 flight test program, and as can be seen in this photo, its fin cap has been removed. It has been rumored for many months that this aircraft, or at least one of the four B-1A prototypes, will be turned over to the USAF Museum at Wright-Patterson AFB, for permanent static display.

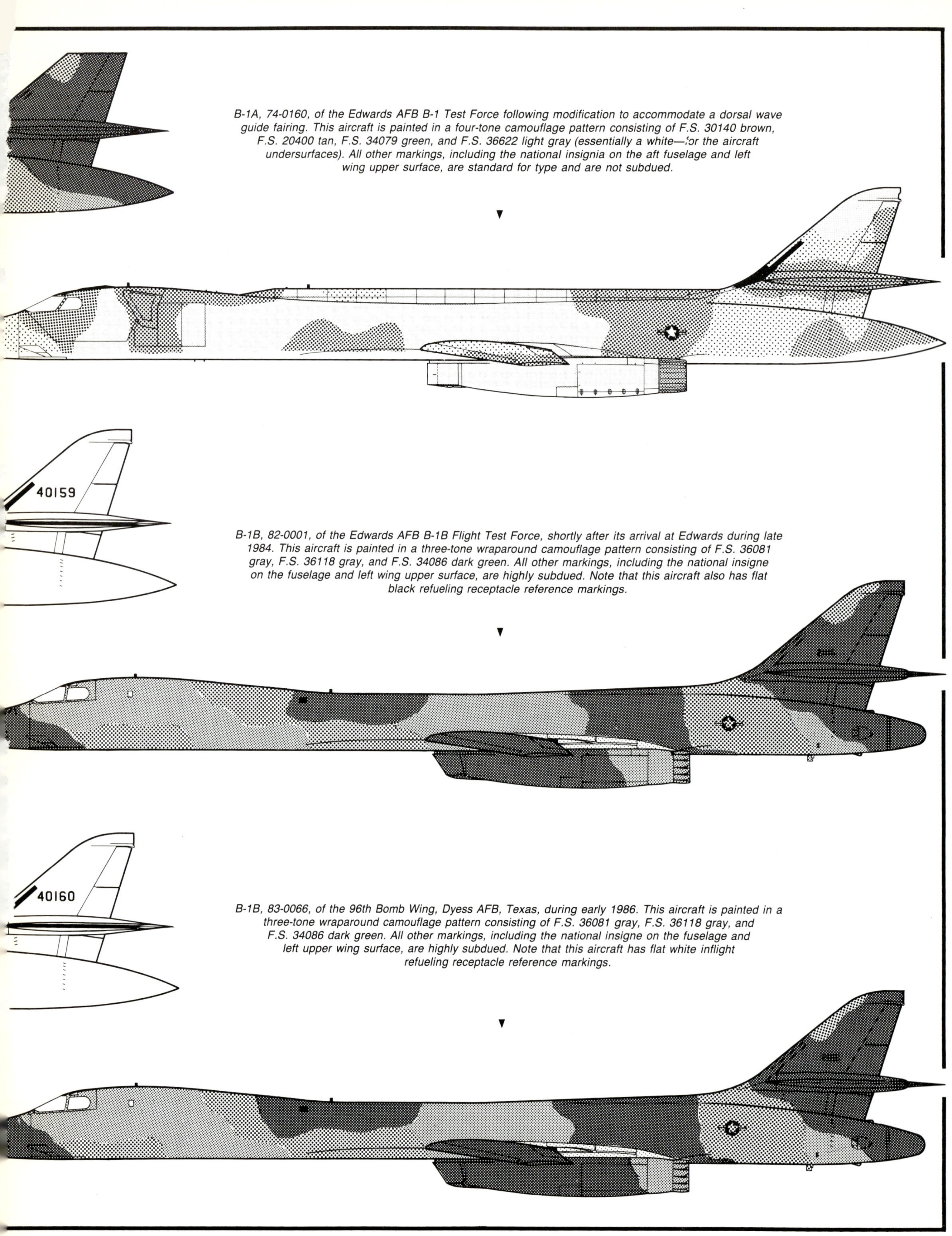

B-1A, 74-0160, of the Edwards AFB B-1 Test Force following modification to accommodate a dorsal wave guide fairing. This aircraft is painted in a four-tone camouflage pattern consisting of F.S. 30140 brown, F.S. 20400 tan, F.S. 34079 green, and F.S. 36622 light gray (essentially a white—for the aircraft undersurfaces). All other markings, including the national insignia on the aft fuselage and left wing upper surface, are standard for type and are not subdued.

B-1B, 82-0001, of the Edwards AFB B-1B Flight Test Force, shortly after its arrival at Edwards during late 1984. This aircraft is painted in a three-tone wraparound camouflage pattern consisting of F.S. 36081 gray, F.S. 36118 gray, and F.S. 34086 dark green. All other markings, including the national insigne on the fuselage and left wing upper surface, are highly subdued. Note that this aircraft also has flat black refueling receptacle reference markings.

B-1B, 83-0066, of the 96th Bomb Wing, Dyess AFB, Texas, during early 1986. This aircraft is painted in a three-tone wraparound camouflage pattern consisting of F.S. 36081 gray, F.S. 36118 gray, and F.S. 34086 dark green. All other markings, including the national insigne on the fuselage and left upper wing surface, are highly subdued. Note that this aircraft has flat white inflight refueling receptacle reference markings.

SELECT MARKINGS

Drawn by Douglas Slowiak   **Scale: 1/200th**

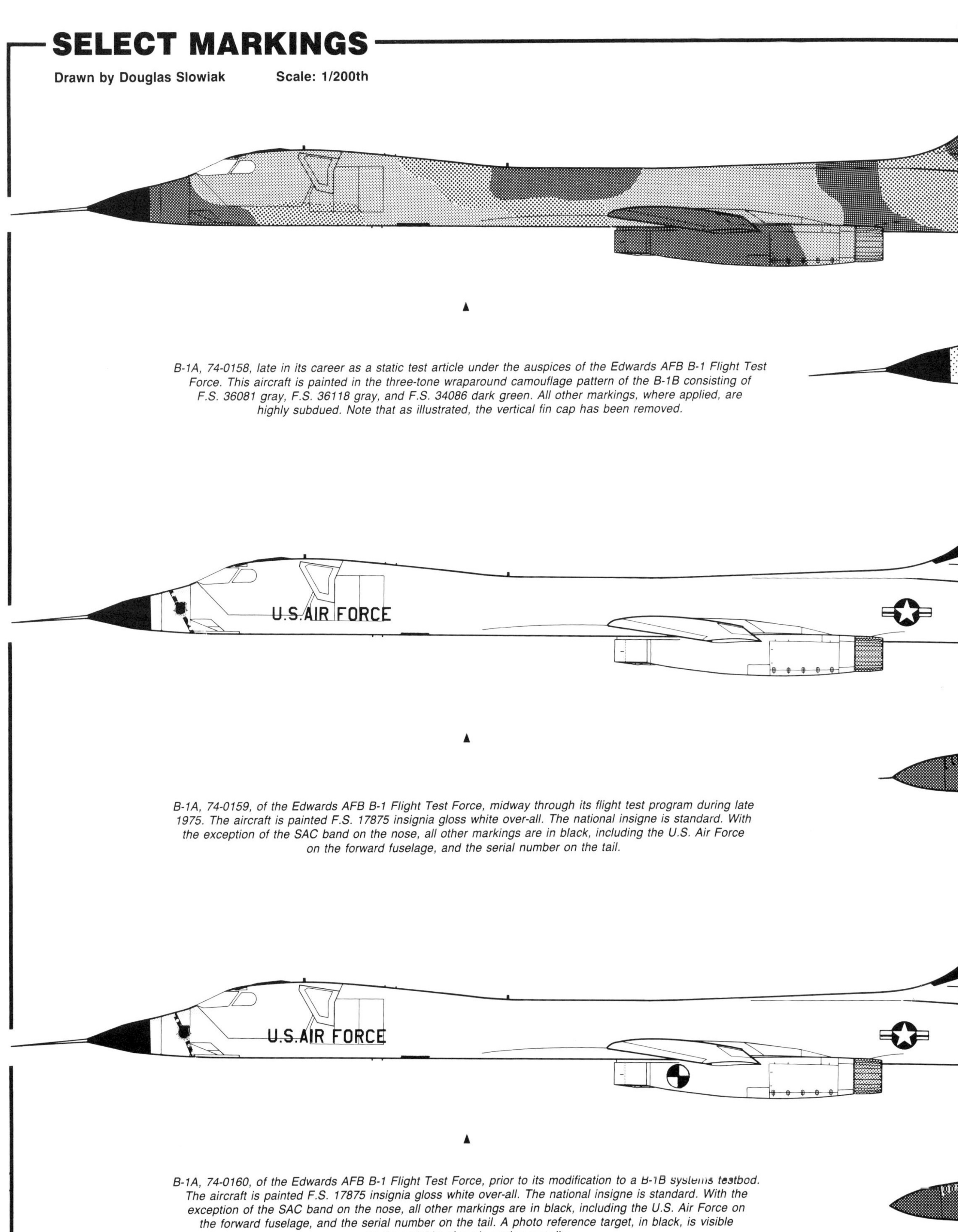

B-1A, 74-0158, late in its career as a static test article under the auspices of the Edwards AFB B-1 Flight Test Force. This aircraft is painted in the three-tone wraparound camouflage pattern of the B-1B consisting of F.S. 36081 gray, F.S. 36118 gray, and F.S. 34086 dark green. All other markings, where applied, are highly subdued. Note that as illustrated, the vertical fin cap has been removed.

B-1A, 74-0159, of the Edwards AFB B-1 Flight Test Force, midway through its flight test program during late 1975. The aircraft is painted F.S. 17875 insignia gloss white over-all. The national insigne is standard. With the exception of the SAC band on the nose, all other markings are in black, including the U.S. Air Force on the forward fuselage, and the serial number on the tail.

B-1A, 74-0160, of the Edwards AFB B-1 Flight Test Force, prior to its modification to a B-1B systems testbed. The aircraft is painted F.S. 17875 insignia gloss white over-all. The national insigne is standard. With the exception of the SAC band on the nose, all other markings are in black, including the U.S. Air Force on the forward fuselage, and the serial number on the tail. A photo reference target, in black, is visible on the outside of each engine nacelle.

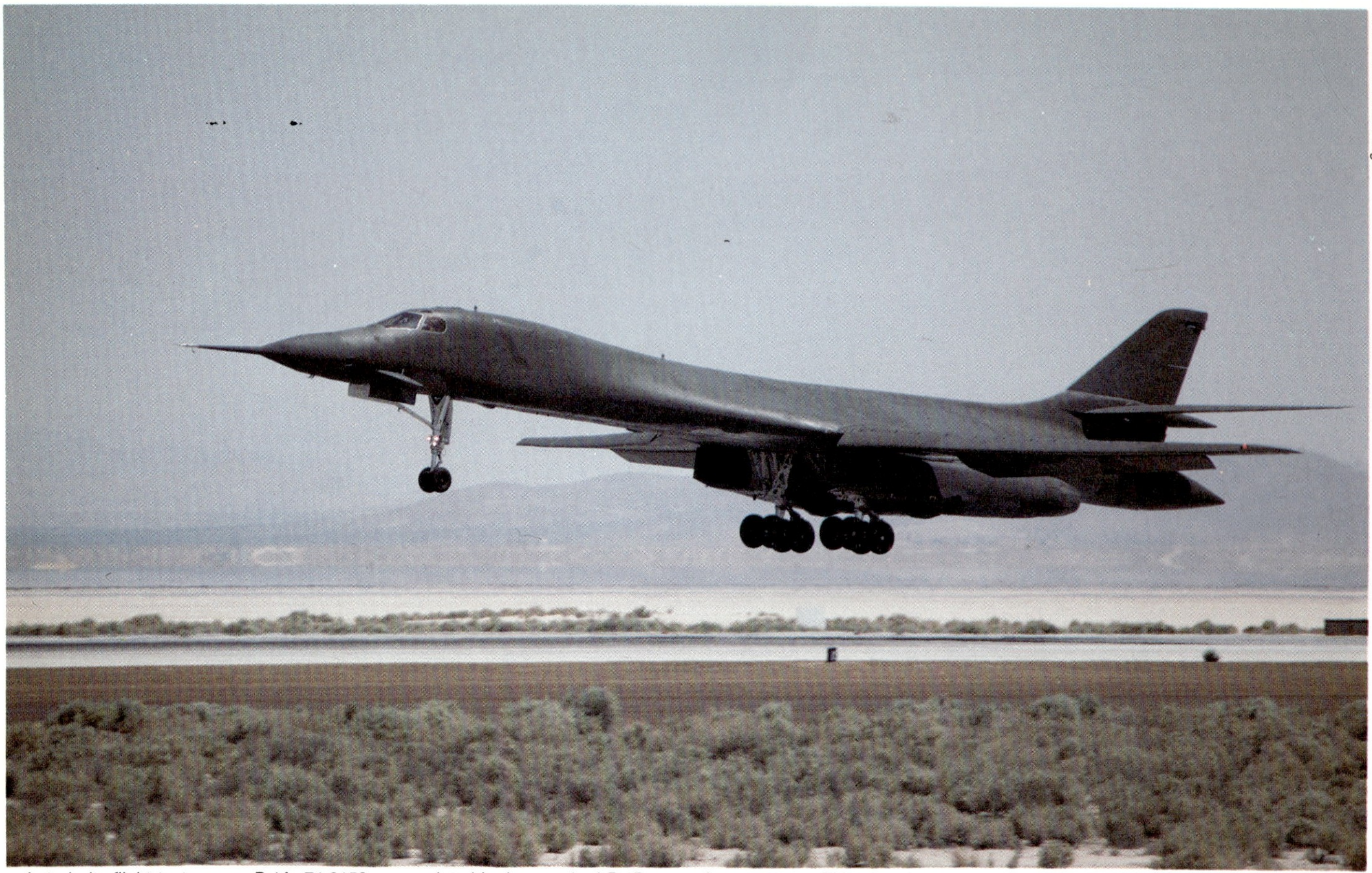

Paul Minert via Don Logan

Late in its flight test career, B-1A, 74-0159, was painted in the standard B-1B camouflage scheme. This aircraft also was modified to accommodate various B-1B subsystems (mainly flight controls) and was one of two B-1A's chosen to remain airworthy under the auspices of the B-1B flight test program. On August 29, 1984, this aircraft crashed at Edwards AFB and was totally destroyed. The accident cause was later traced to a fuel distribution/c.g. anomaly.

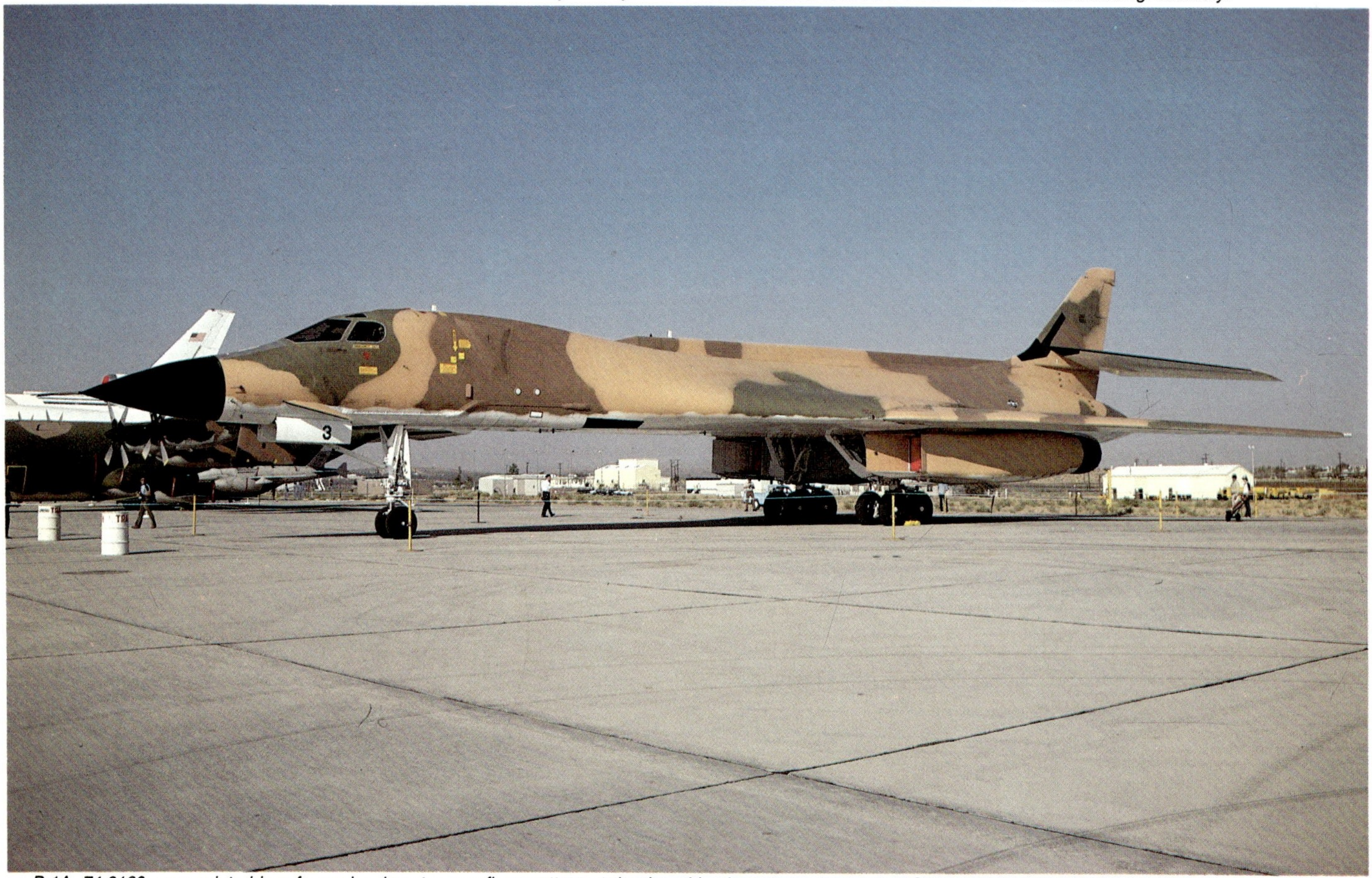

Toshiki Kudo

B-1A, 74-0160, was painted in a four-color desert camouflage pattern at the time this photo was taken during October, 1980. This scheme had been preceded by an all-white scheme, typical of the B-1A test fleet as first flown. When this photo was taken, 74-0160, was equipped with the early Kuras-Alterman "Crosseye" ECM monopulse wave guide assembly in the form of a dorsal spine. A similar wave guide assembly is now located in the bomb bay areas of the B-1B.

R. E. Arance via Craig Kaston

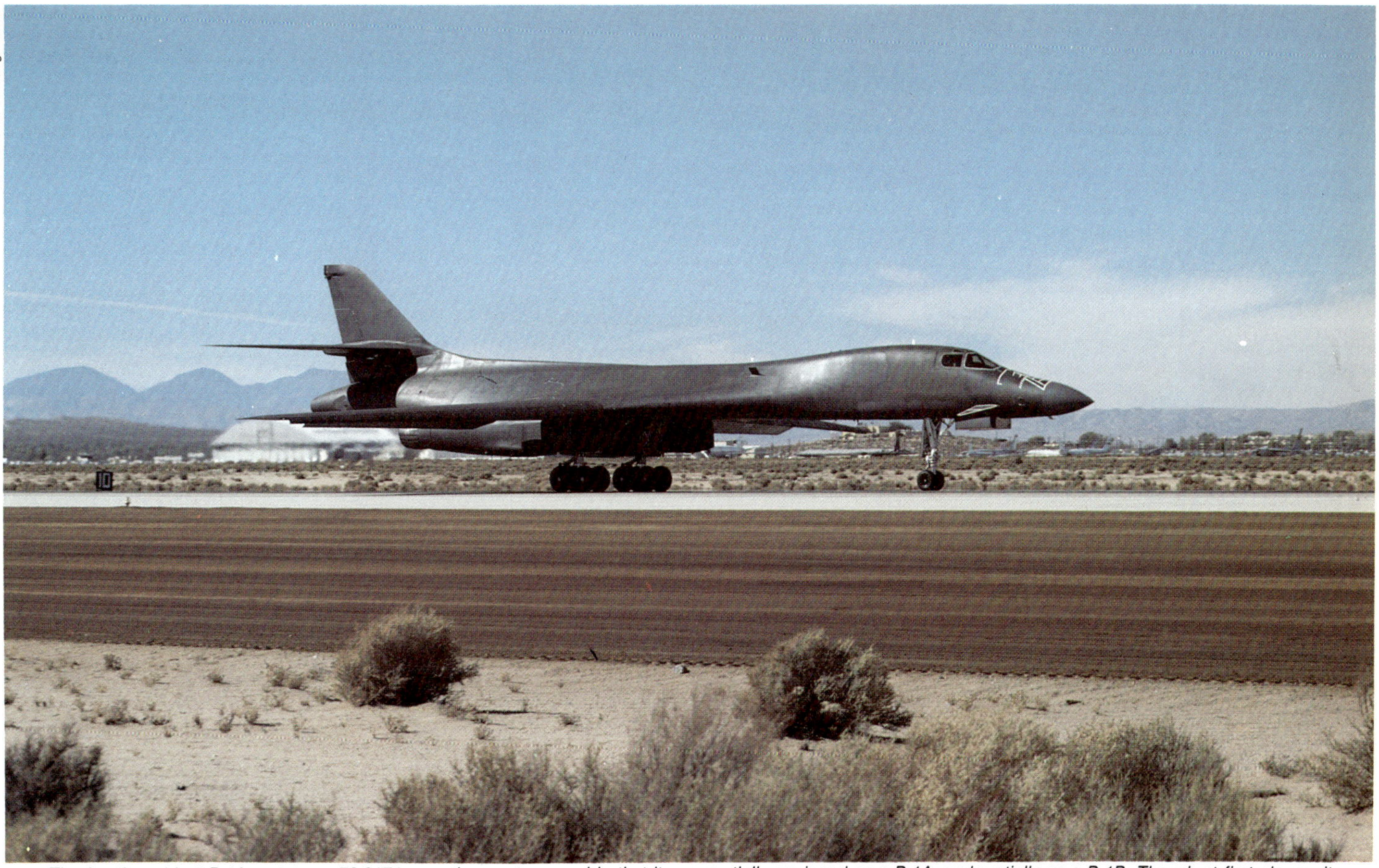

The fourth and last B-1A prototype, 76-0174, was the most unusual in that it was partially equipped as a B-1A, and partially as a B-1B. Though at first glance, it appears to be a B-1B, it does not have such details as the reconfigured B-1B-type intake ramps, the observation windows for the DSO and OSO stations, and the B-1B's shorter exhaust nozzles. It remains active as a B-1B flight test article at Edwards AFB.

Jay Miller/Aerofax, Inc.

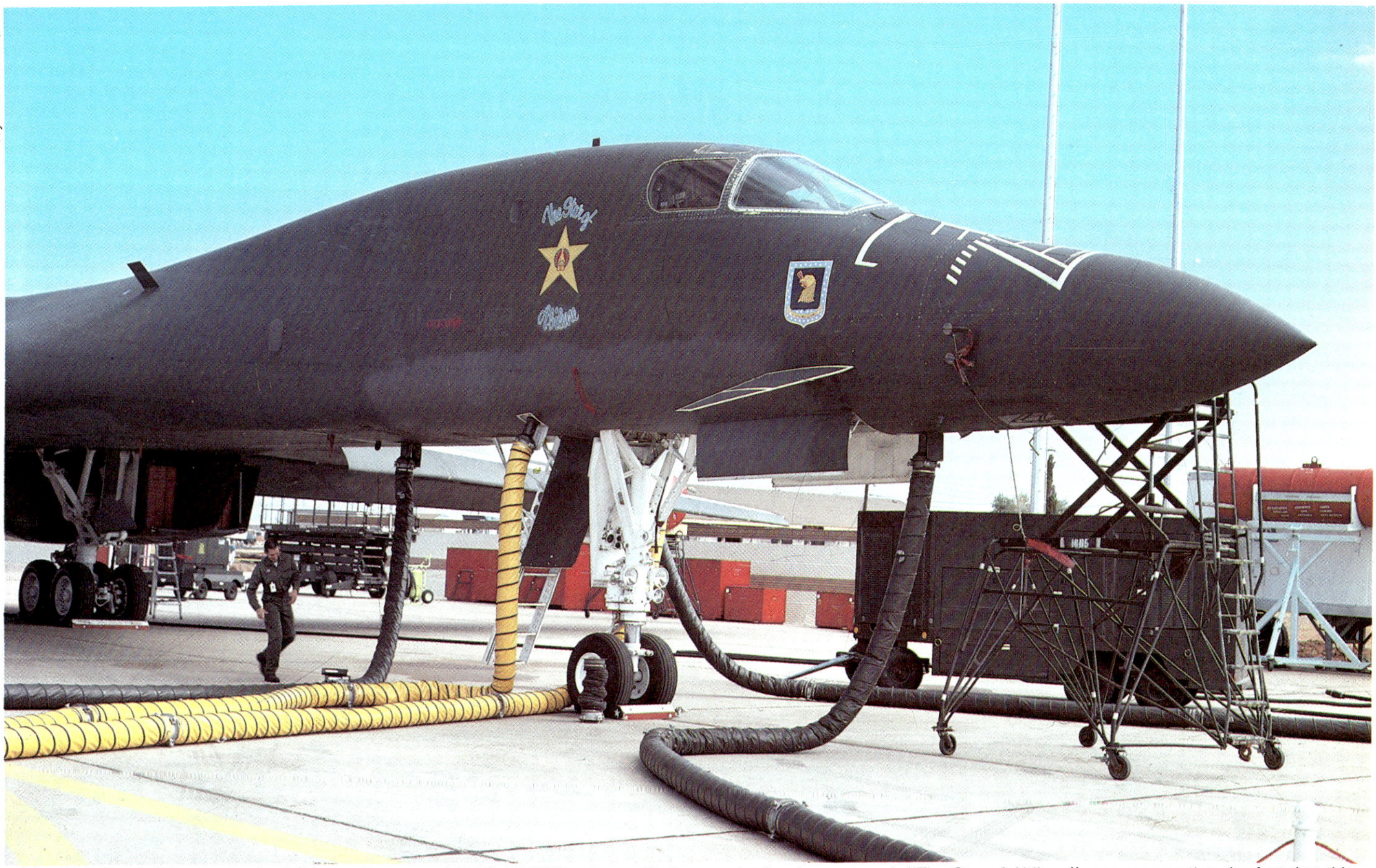

The 96th Bomb Wing badge is visible on the nose of B-1B, 83-0065, along with the special fuselage art work "The Star of Abilene", commemorating the fact that this was the first operational B-1B to be assigned to the base. Visible also are the four flexible air-conditioning ducts. The white visual alignment markings are for night inflight refueling requirements. These will eventually go to a revised, light gray scheme to make them less visible.

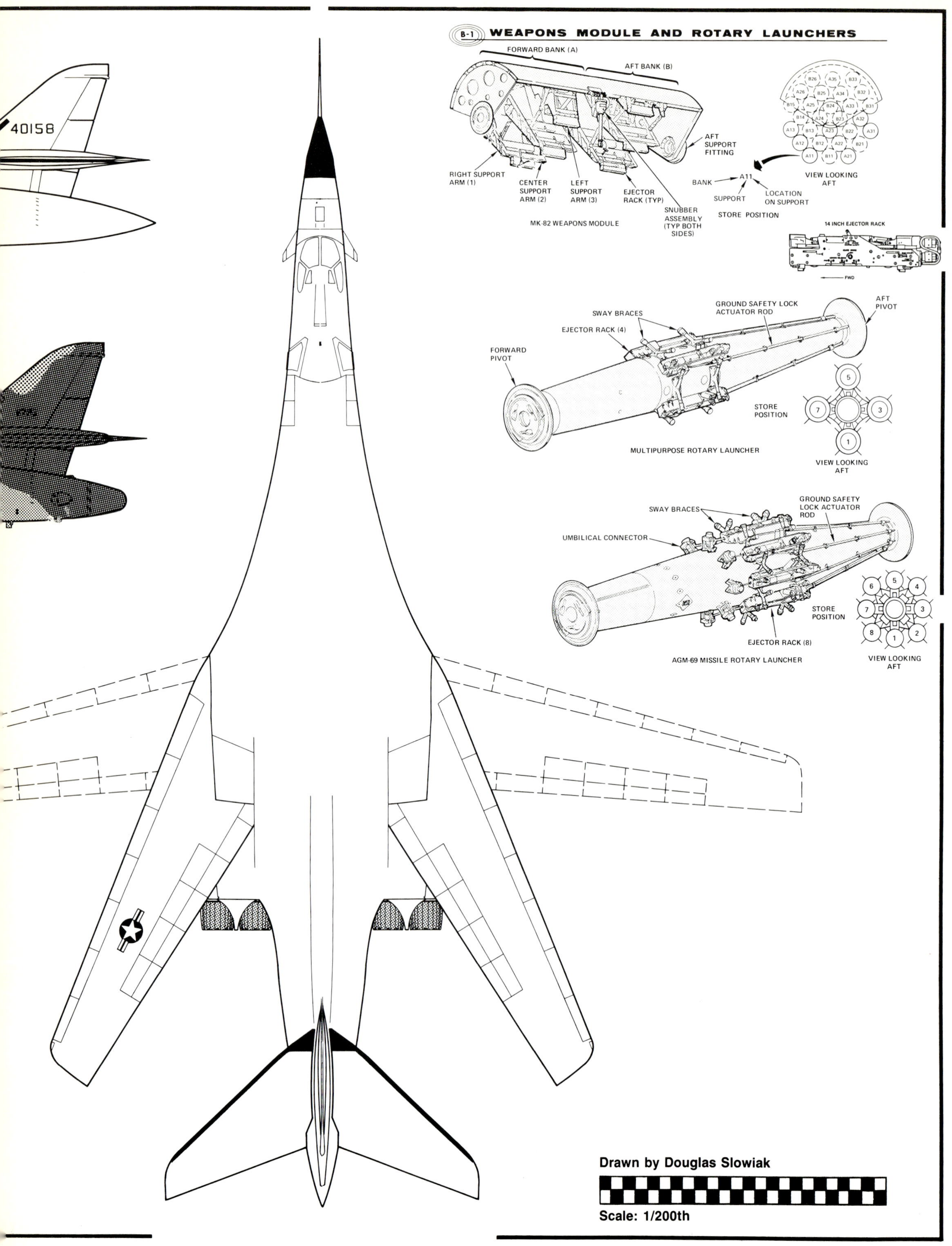

40158
B-1 WEAPONS MODULE AND ROTARY LAUNCHERS
FORWARD BANK (A)
AFT BANK (B)
AFT SUPPORT FITTING
RIGHT SUPPORT ARM (1)
CENTER SUPPORT ARM (2)
LEFT SUPPORT ARM (3)
EJECTOR RACK (TYP)
SNUBBER ASSEMBLY (TYP BOTH SIDES)
BANK
SUPPORT
A11
LOCATION ON SUPPORT
STORE POSITION
VIEW LOOKING AFT
MK-82 WEAPONS MODULE
14 INCH EJECTOR RACK
FWD
SWAY BRACES
EJECTOR RACK (4)
GROUND SAFETY LOCK ACTUATOR ROD
AFT PIVOT
FORWARD PIVOT
STORE POSITION
MULTIPURPOSE ROTARY LAUNCHER
VIEW LOOKING AFT
SWAY BRACES
GROUND SAFETY LOCK ACTUATOR ROD
UMBILICAL CONNECTOR
STORE POSITION
EJECTOR RACK (8)
AGM-69 MISSILE ROTARY LAUNCHER
VIEW LOOKING AFT
Drawn by Douglas Slowiak
Scale: 1/200th

ROCKWELL INTERNATIONAL
B-1A, 74-0158

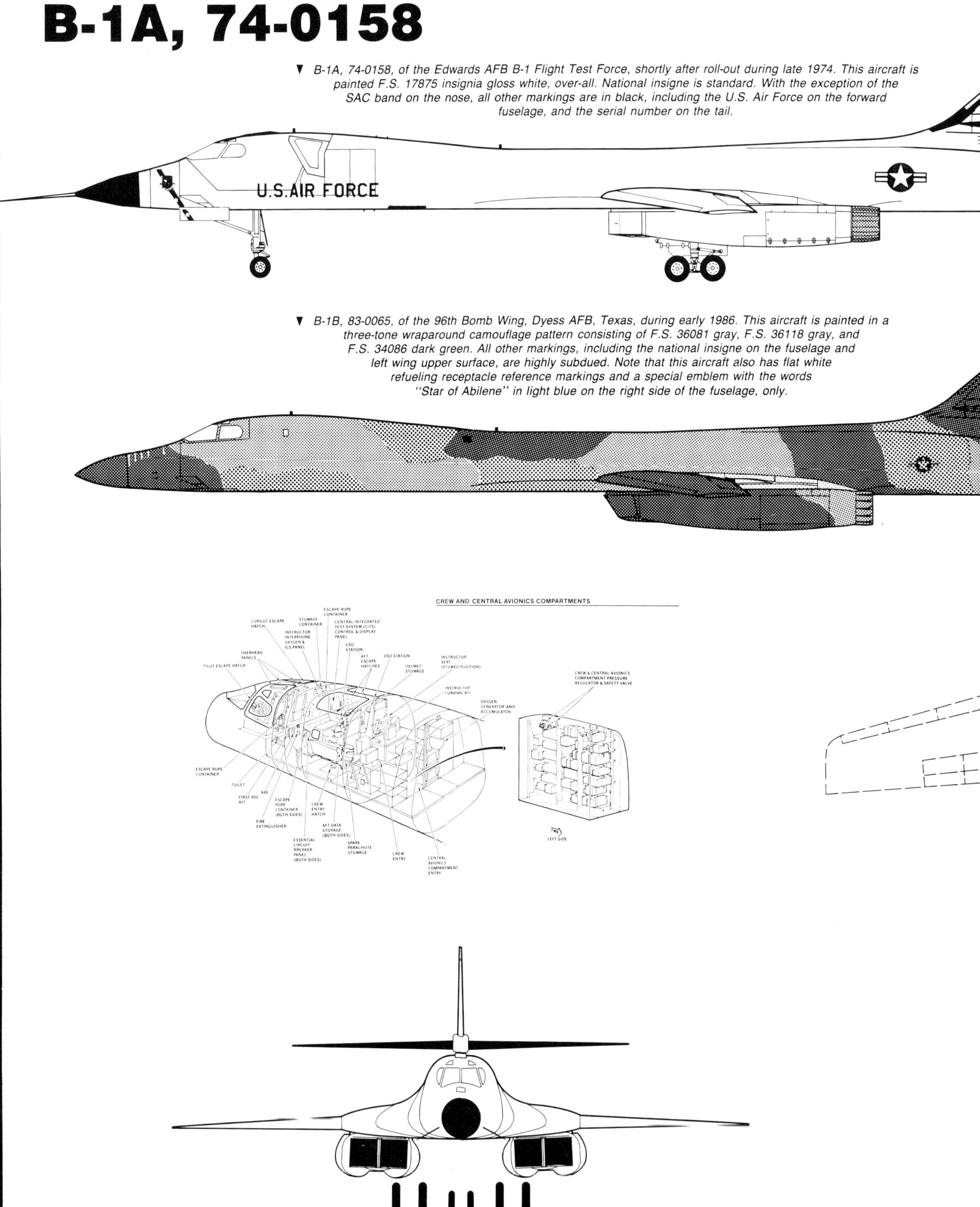

▼ B-1A, 74-0158, of the Edwards AFB B-1 Flight Test Force, shortly after roll-out during late 1974. This aircraft is painted F.S. 17875 insignia gloss white, over-all. National insigne is standard. With the exception of the SAC band on the nose, all other markings are in black, including the U.S. Air Force on the forward fuselage, and the serial number on the tail.

▼ B-1B, 83-0065, of the 96th Bomb Wing, Dyess AFB, Texas, during early 1986. This aircraft is painted in a three-tone wraparound camouflage pattern consisting of F.S. 36081 gray, F.S. 36118 gray, and F.S. 34086 dark green. All other markings, including the national insigne on the fuselage and left wing upper surface, are highly subdued. Note that this aircraft also has flat white refueling receptacle reference markings and a special emblem with the words "Star of Abilene" in light blue on the right side of the fuselage, only.

Brian Rogers

B-1B, 83-0066, during a temporary stopover at Carswell AFB, Texas. The temporary Carswell visit by the aircraft proved an ideal opportunity for SAC personnel stationed there to view the aircraft first hand. Carswell, due to its proximity to Dyess AFB, is often used for B-1B touch-and-go practice. With an ever-growing B-1B population at Dyess, Carswell appearances will almost certainly increase in number.

Jay Miller/Aerofax, Inc.

The B-1B's main instrument panel is fairly conventional and does not incorporate a particularly high percentage of high tech instrumentation options. Most of the instrumentation is, in fact, of the conventional analogue variety, though there are some vertical displays and two primary CRT's. Unusually, for a bomber, there are also two throttle quadrants—one for the pilot and one for the co-pilot. That for the pilot is mounted on the left cockpit wall console.

Rockwell International

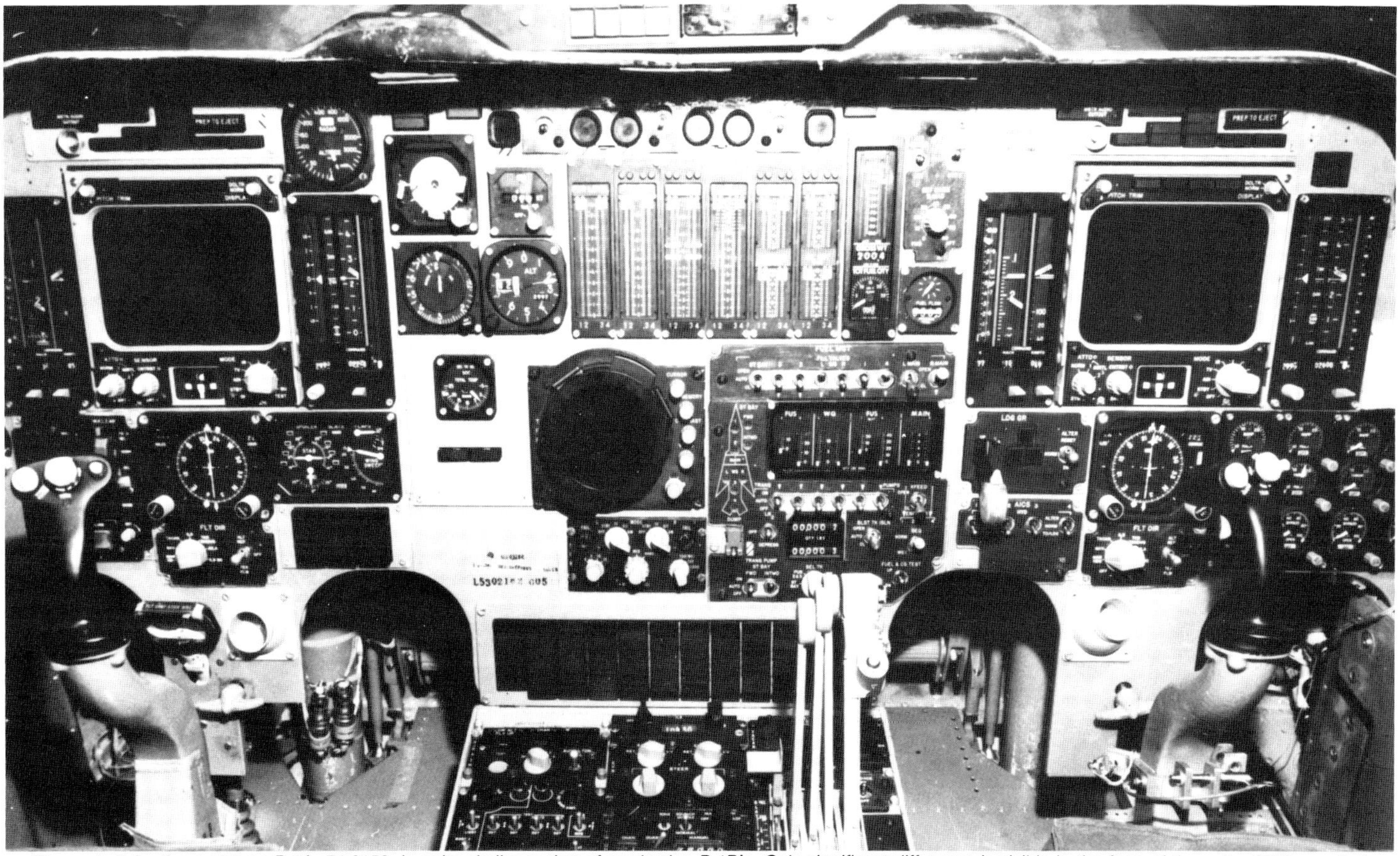

The cockpit for the prototype B-1A, 74-0158, is quite similar to that of production B-1B's. Only significant difference is visible in the form of the radar CRT mounted near the center of the main console. This is not installed on production aircraft. Other minor differences include instrumentation size and type, knob designs, and vertical display graphics. Though not visible in photo, the B-1A's did not have individual ejection seats but rather an encapsulated ejection system.

Jay Miller/Aerofax, Inc.

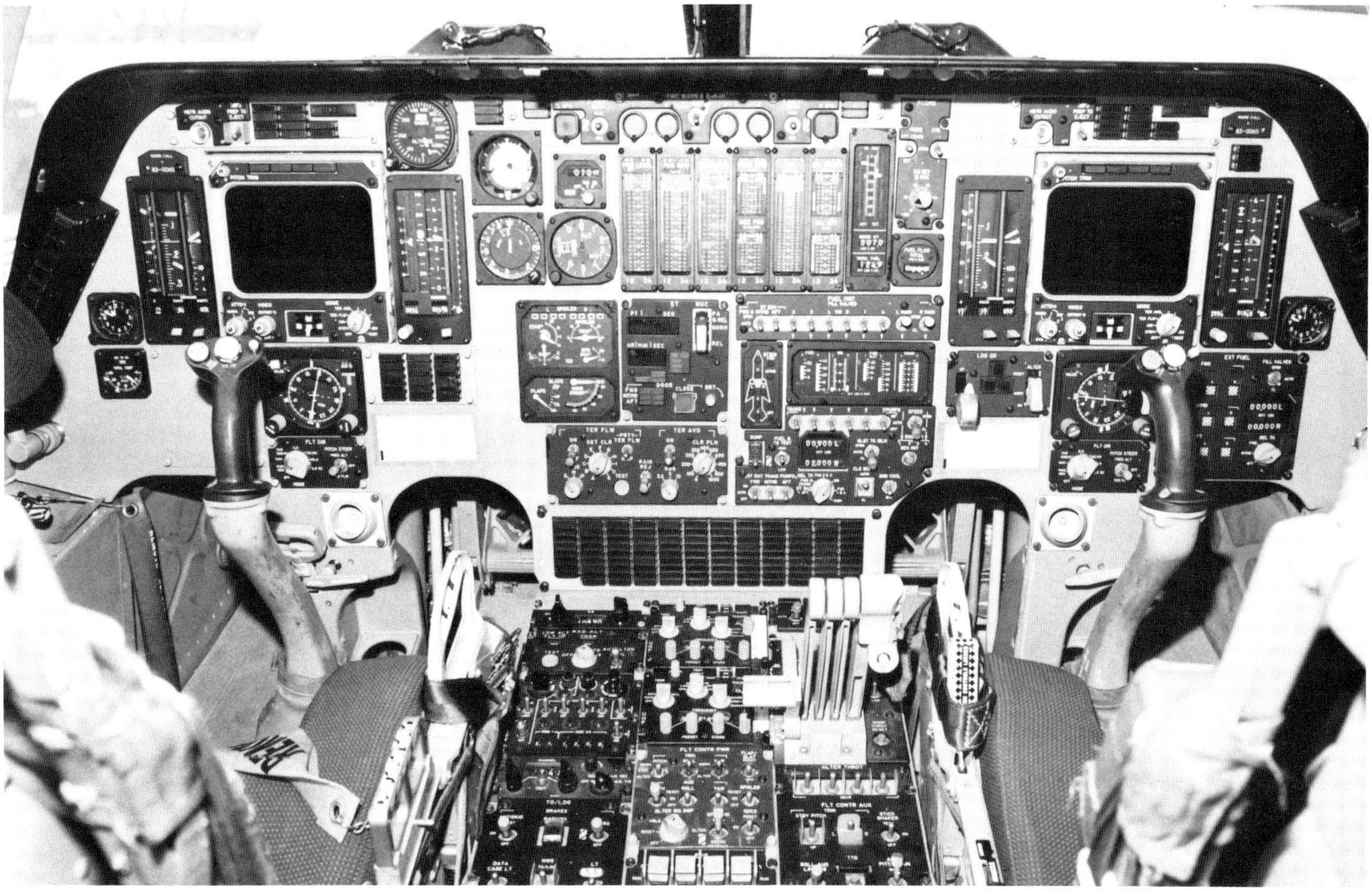

B-1B, 83-0065, cockpit is representative of the production configuration. Very few digital displays are provided in the form of instrumentation, though the CRT's provide the information normally provided by analogue flight attitude systems. Unlike the B-1A's, the B-1B cockpit is also equipped with conventional ejection seats, these dictating major design changes in the cockpit structure and emergency egress procedures. Noteworthy in photo is the co-pilot's throttle quadrant.

Rockwell International

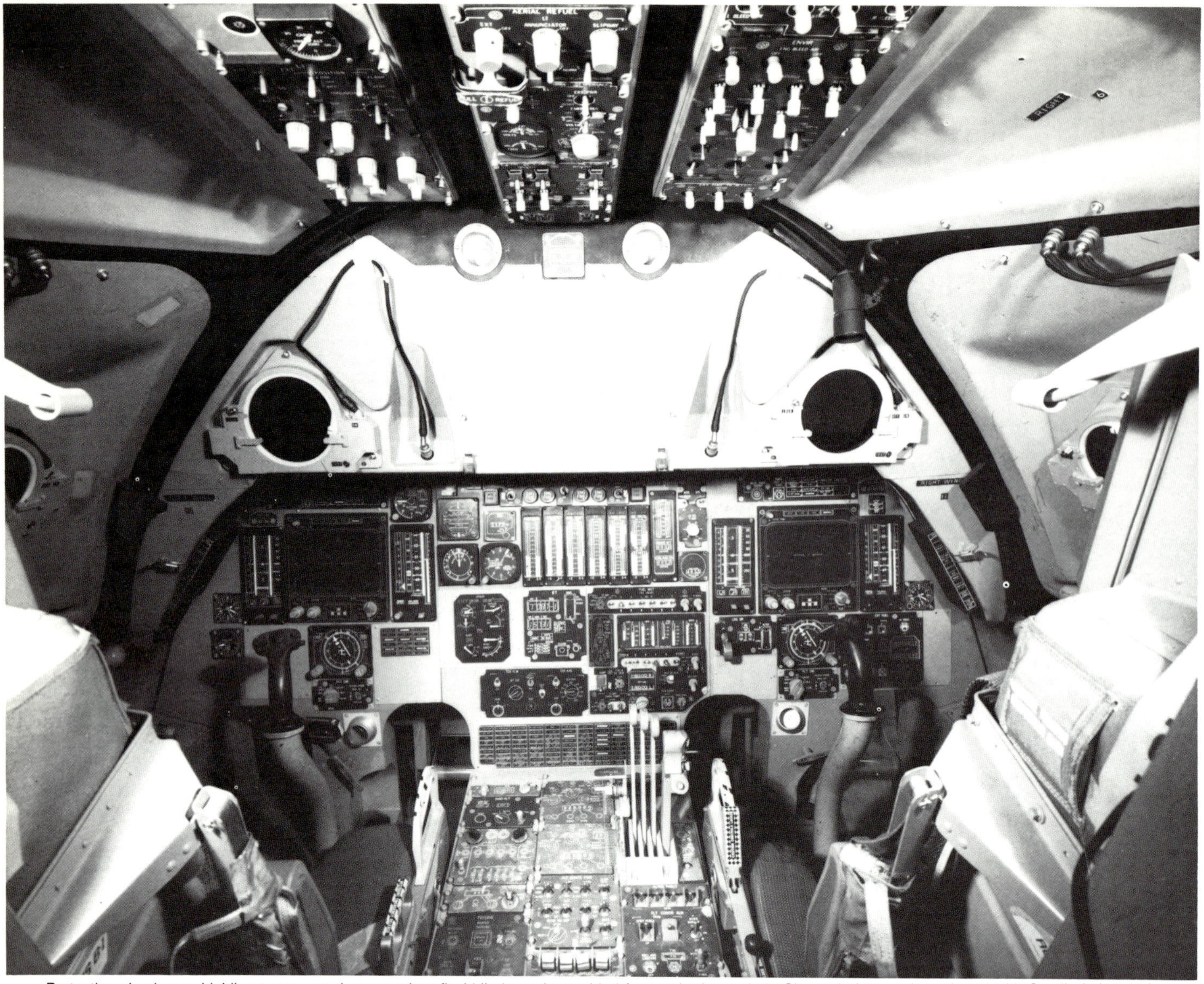

Protective aluminum shielding to prevent thermonuclear flashblindness is provided for use in the cockpit. Six portholes, each equipped with Sandia Laboratories developed PLZT (Polarized Lead Zercomnium Titanate) ceramic glass elements that electro-optically reduce external light to .003% of its original intensity in 150 microseconds, are provided for external vision.

Jay Miller/Aerofax, Inc.

Jay Miller/Aerofax, Inc.

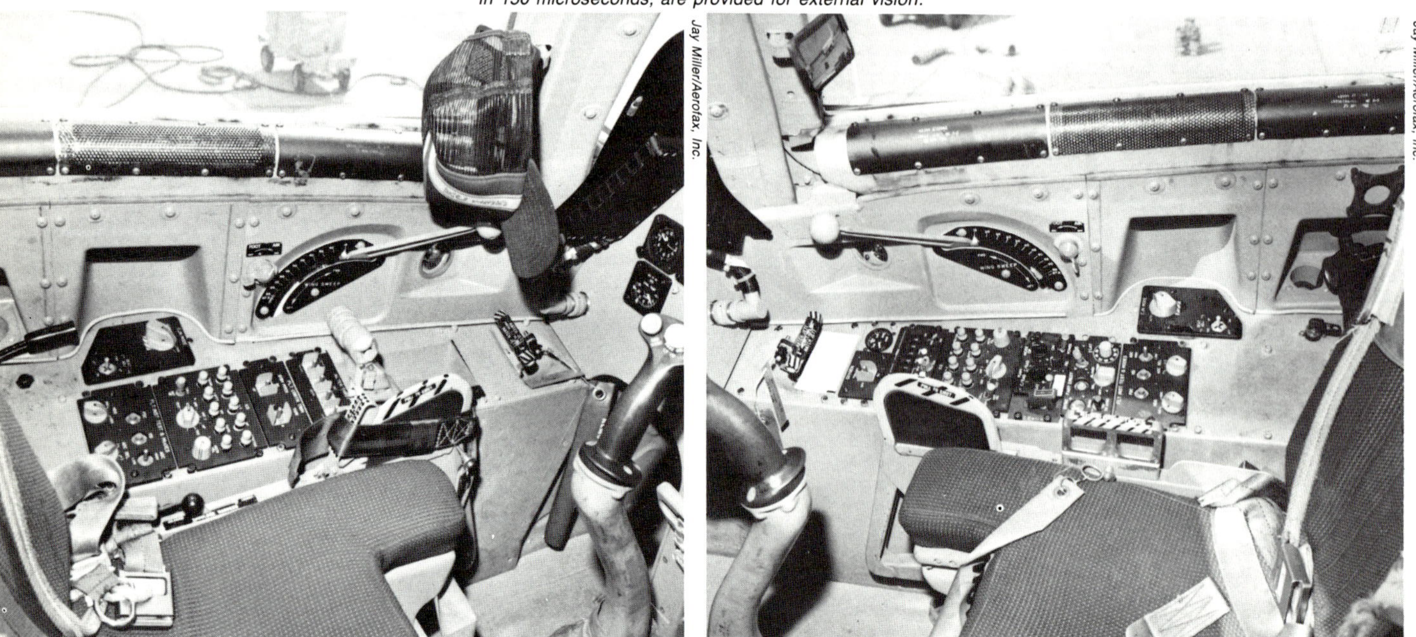

The pilot's left cockpit wall console (left) serves as the mounting point for the pilot's wing sweep handle, the pilot's throttle quadrant, and several test and trim control system panels. The co-pilot's right cockpit wall console (right) serves as the mounting point for the co-pilot's wing sweep handle, oxygen regulation, some communications equipment, and miscellaneous navigation system panels.

Jay Miller/Aerofax, Inc.

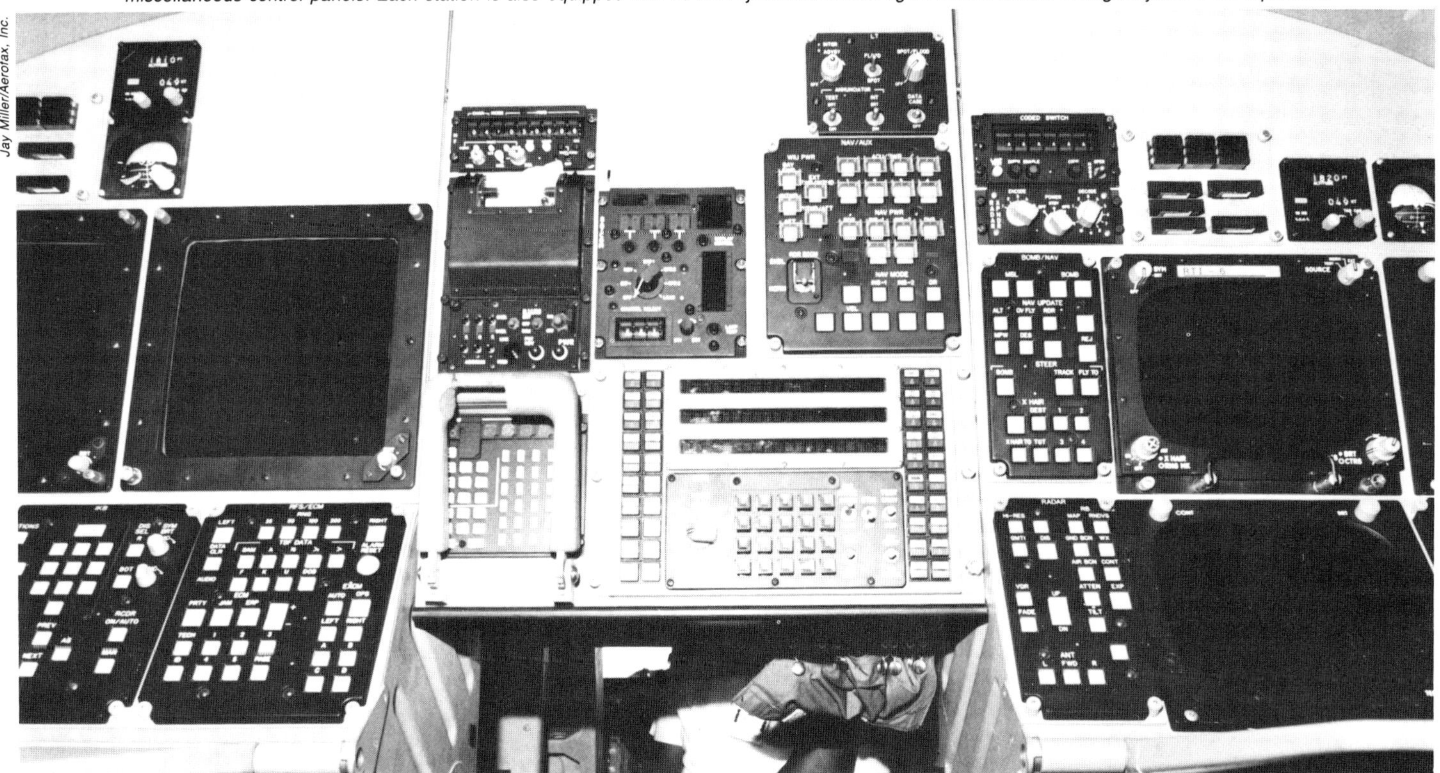

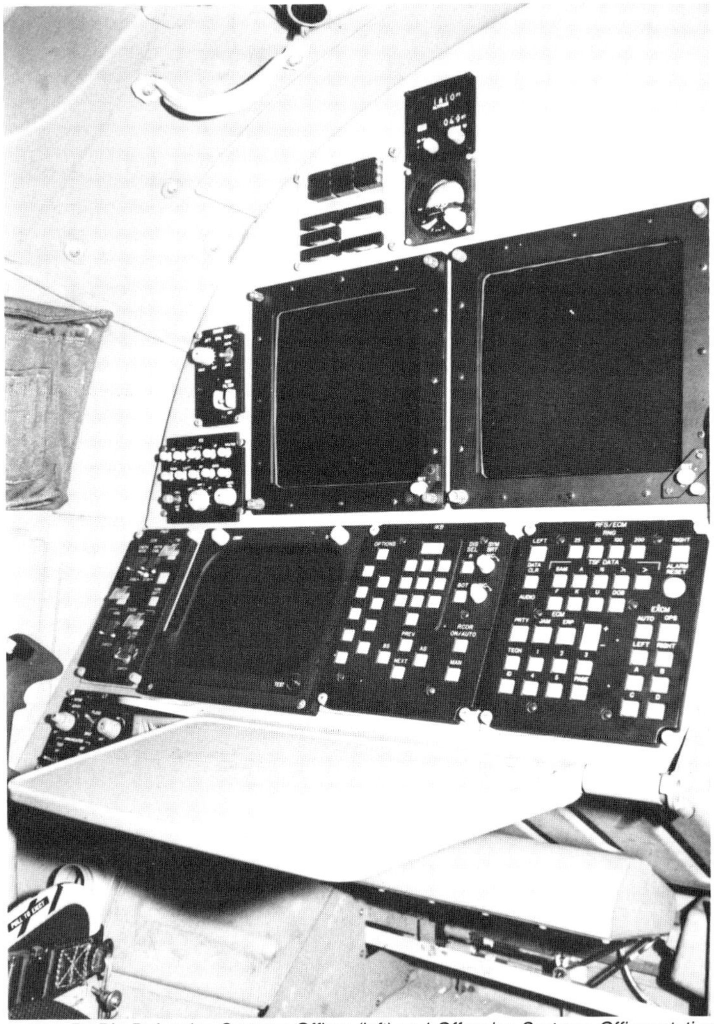

Jay Miller/Aerofax, Inc.

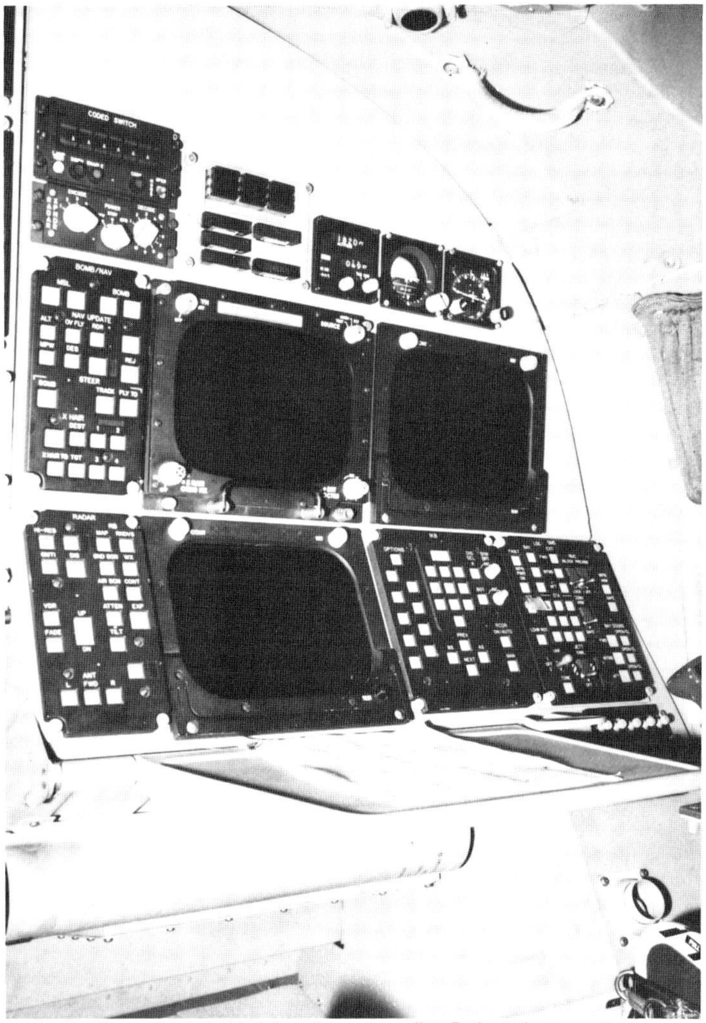

The B-1B's Defensive Systems Officer (left) and Offensive Systems Officer stations are located immediately behind the pilot and co-pilot. Both stations are dominated by CRT's that display complex information formats related to defensive and offensive systems respectively. Each station is equipped with a folding table and miscellaneous control panels. Each station is also equipped with its own ejection seat that egresses the aircraft through a jettisonable top hatch.

Jay Miller/Aerofax, Inc.

The center panel, located between the DSO and OSO stations, accommodates sub-panels that support the inertial navigation system, the satellite communications system, and the Central Integrated Test System (CITS). The latter, which is a fall-out system from the Rockwell Space Shuttle program and which was originally scheduled for pre-production test aircraft only, is now a standard production item. It's ability to locate system failures and other related discrepancies is excellent.

Boeing, under sub-contract to Rockwell, is building a series of OSO training units. Shown is an early study mock-up utilizing pre-production offensive system design concepts. The panel provides screens for multi-function displays, the forward-looking radar and i.r. systems, and stores management information.

B-1B entry is through a retractable ladder and cover hatch located to the rear of the nose gear. The hatch can be jettisoned for emergency egress.

PILOT/COPILOT AND CENTER INSTRUMENT PANELS

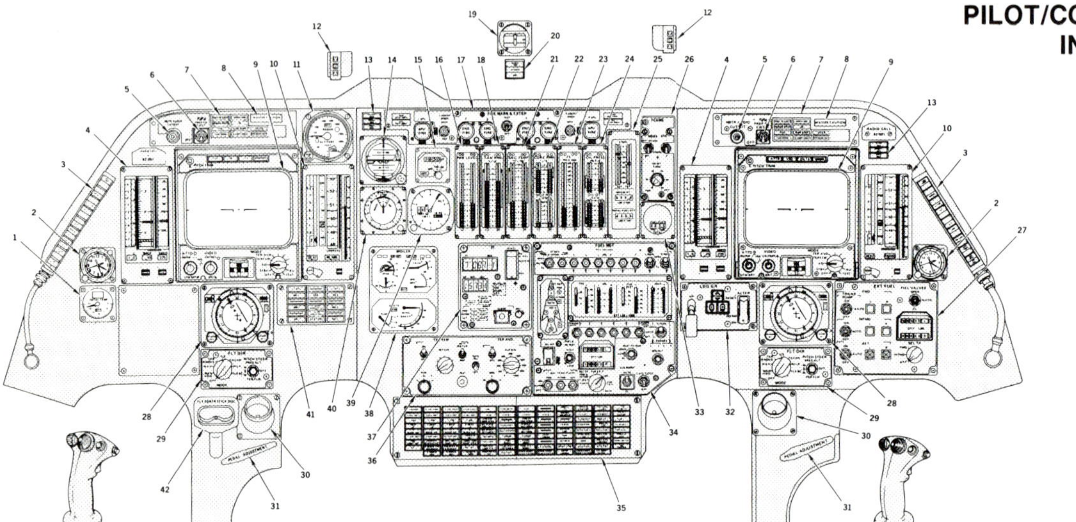

1. Total Temperature Indicator
2. Clock
3. Automatic Flight Control System Control Panel
4. Airspeed/Mach Indicator
5. Master Audio Cutout Button
6. PREP TO EJECT Switch
7. Master Caution Panel
8. Master Caution Light
9. Vertical Situation Display
10. Altitude/Vertical Velocity Indicator
11. Radar Altimeter
12. Angle-of-Attack/Indexer Indicator
13. Marker Beacon Lights
14. Standby Attitude Indicator
15. Groundspeed/True Airspeed Indicator
16. Engine Power Level Indicator
17. Fire Warning and Extinguisher Control Panel
18. Engine Fan RPM Indicator
19. Standby Compass
20. Air Refuel/Nosewheel Steering Light
21. Engine Temperature Indicator
22. Engine Core RPM and Nozzle Position Indicators
23. Engine Fuel Flow Indicators
24. Engine Oil Pressure and Oil Quantity Indicators
25. Center-of-Gravity Gross Weight/Total Fuel Quantity
26. Fuel and CG Management System Panel
27. External Fuel Control Panel
28. Horizontal Situation Indicator
29. Flight Director Control Panel
30. Conditioned Air Outlet
31. Rudder Pedal Adjustment Handle
32. Landing Gear Control Panel
33. Total Fuel Flow Indicator
34. Fuel Management Panel
35. Main Caution Panel
36. TER FLW/ TER AVD Control Panel
37. Stores Panel
38. Surface Position Indicator
39. Standby Altimeter
40. Standby Airspeed/Mach Indicator
41. Auxiliary Caution Panel
42. Flight Control Stick Disconnect Handle

AFT STATION INSTRUMENT PANELS AND SIDE CONSOLES

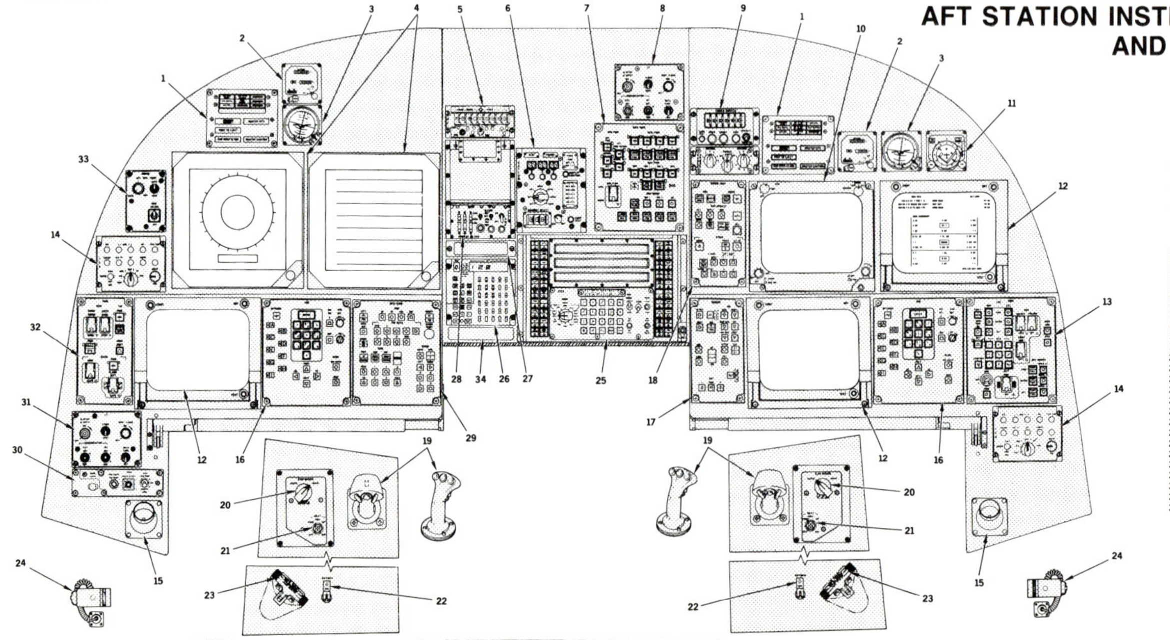

1. DSO/OSO Caution Panel
2. Flight Parameter Indicator
3. Attitude Indicator
4. Electronic Display Unit
5. HF Radio Panel
6. SATCOM Control Panel
7. NAV/AUX Panel
8. OSO Lighting Panel
9. Coded Switch Panel
10. Radar Display Unit
11. Horizontal Situation Panel
12. Multifunction Display
13. Stores Management System Panel
14. Intercom Control System Panel
15. Conditioned Air Outlet
16. Integrated Keyboard
17. Radar Control Panel
18. BOMB/NAV Panel
19. Track Handle
20. EJN MODE Switch
21. Seat Adjustment Switch
22. Oxygen Lever
23. Hatch Jettison
24. Utility Light
25. CITS Panel
26. SATCOM Keyboard
27. SATCOM Keyboard Light
28. SATCOM Printer
29. RFS/ECMS Panel
30. EMUX Control Panel
31. DSO Lighting Panel
32. DSO Power Panel
33. Environmental Control Panel
34. SATCOM Keyboard Wrist Support

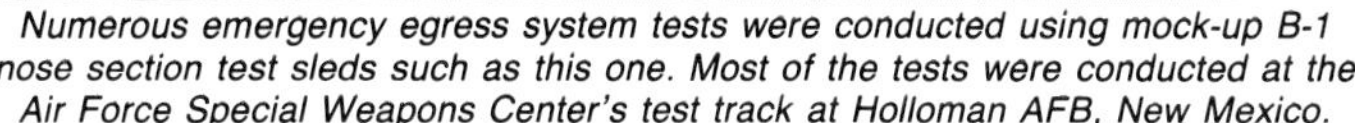

Numerous emergency egress system tests were conducted using mock-up B-1 nose section test sleds such as this one. Most of the tests were conducted at the Air Force Special Weapons Center's test track at Holloman AFB, New Mexico.

The original B-1 concept included an encapsulated ejection system for the crew. A mock-up capsule is shown with its single fixed propulsion rocket and its single gimballed propulsion rocket exposed.

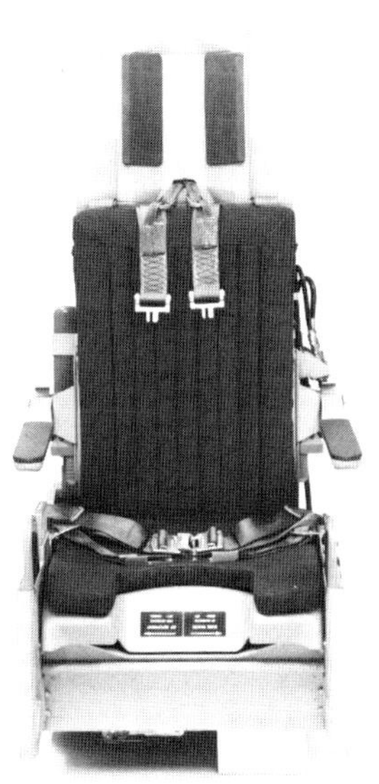

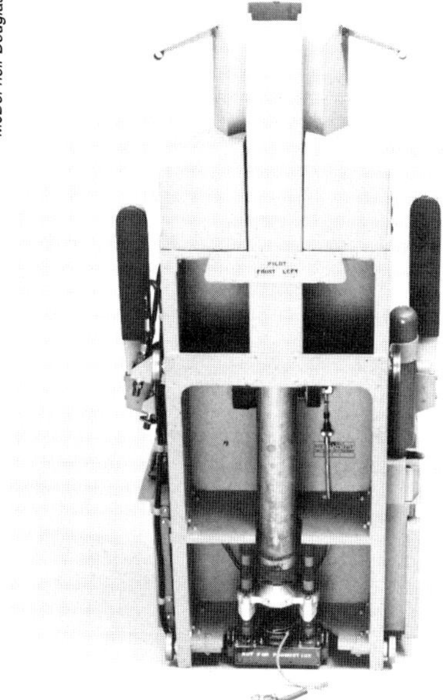

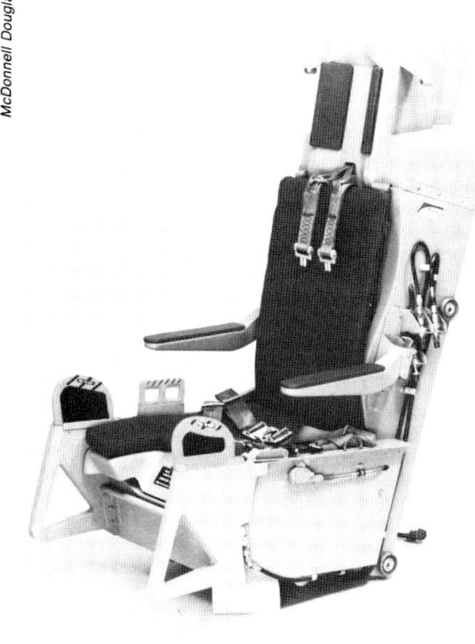

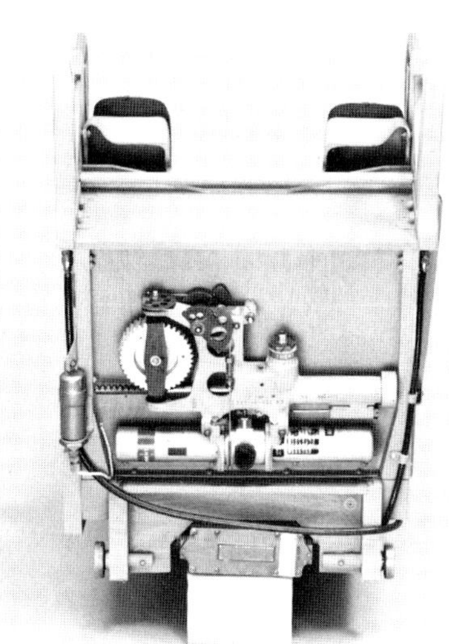

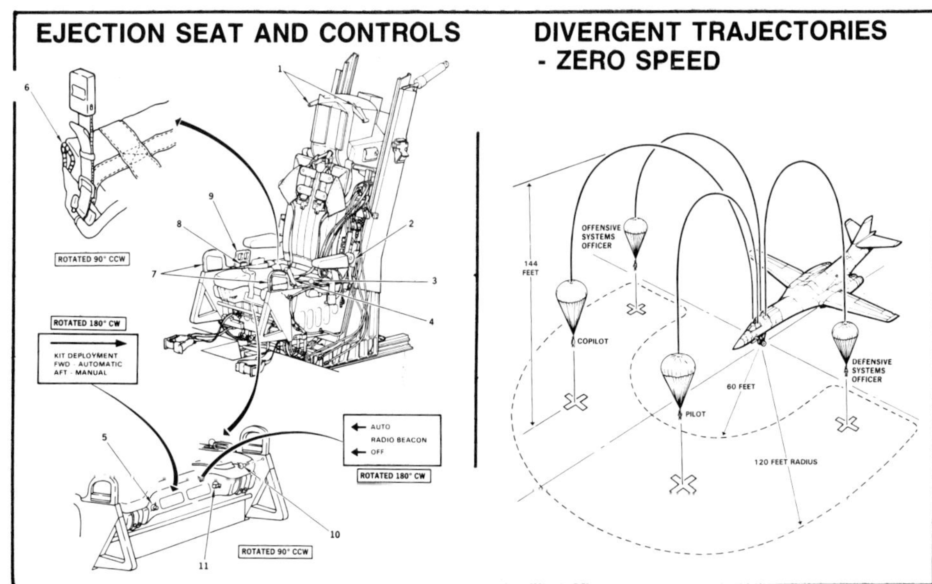

Four views of the B-1B's Advanced Concept Ejection Seat (ACES). The seat permits emergency egress from the B-1B throughout its flight envelope. Unlike fighter-optimized ACES seats, it is equipped with special appendage restraint harnesses and arm rests. The latter are to be removed from operational seats as they have been found to be restrictive during egress situations. The seat shown is a full-scale mock-up equipped with all B-1-related modifications.

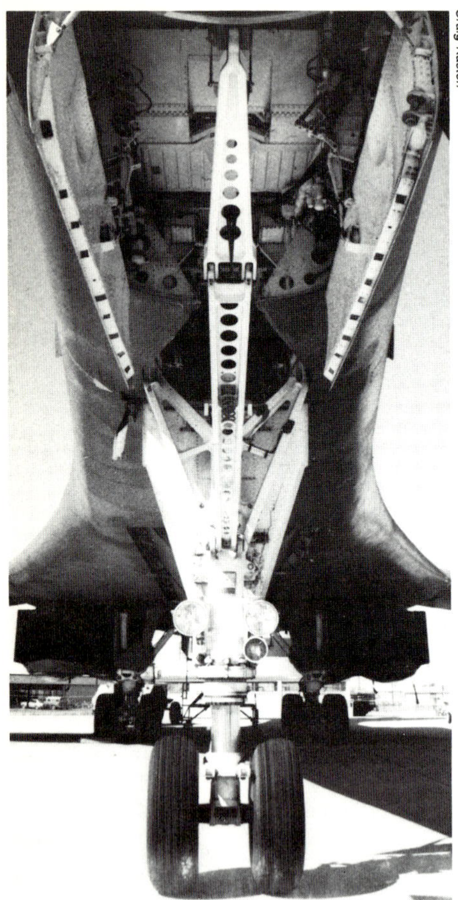

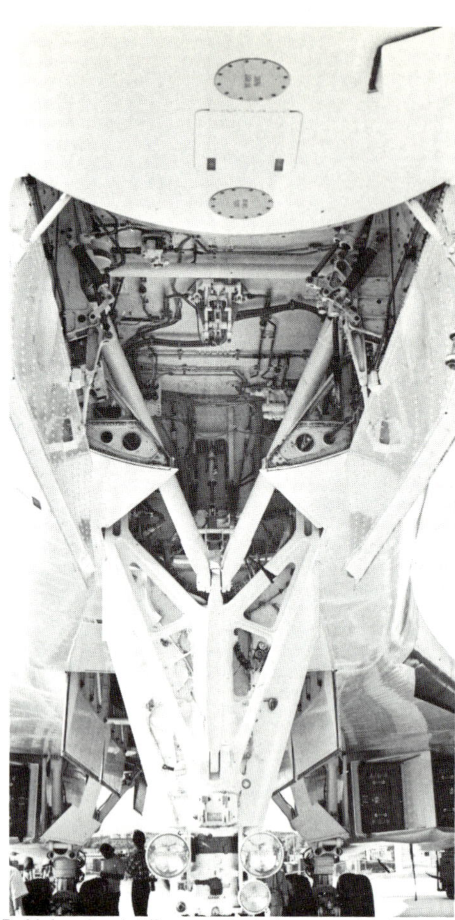

The B-1A's Menasco-manufactured forward retracting nose landing gear differs somewhat from that of the B-1B. Major visual differences include a completely redesigned drag brace strut, minor gear well door shape and assembly changes, and changes to miscellaneous retraction system hardware. The nose gear is steerable (75° to either side) from the cockpit using differential rudder pedal movement. Construction is of both steel and aluminum.

The B-1B's nose landing gear, also manufactured by Menasco, is somewhat lighter than its predecessor. Major changes include a revised drag brace strut design, and minor changes to miscellaneous retraction assemblies. The nose gear well door is hinged where it comes in contact with the fuselage and is attached to the nose gear strut with two small connecting rods. A combination of three landing/taxi lightes are attached to the main strut assembly.

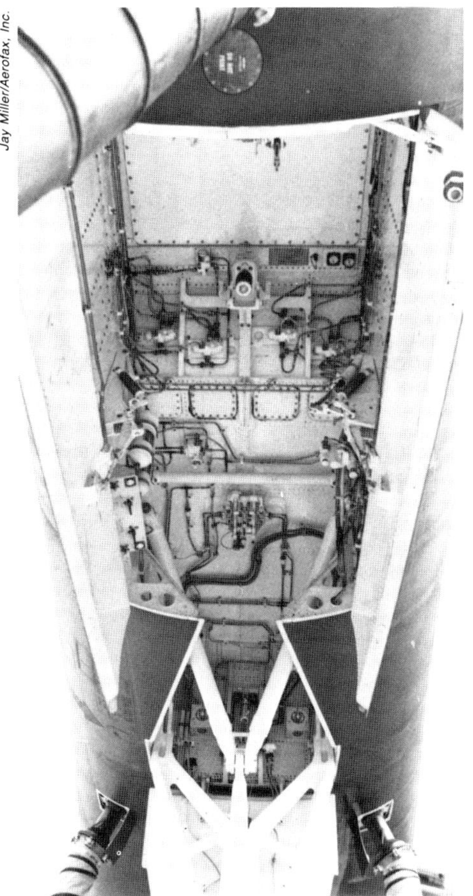

View looking aft into the nose gear retraction well. Two hydraulic actuators fold the gear forward during the retraction process.

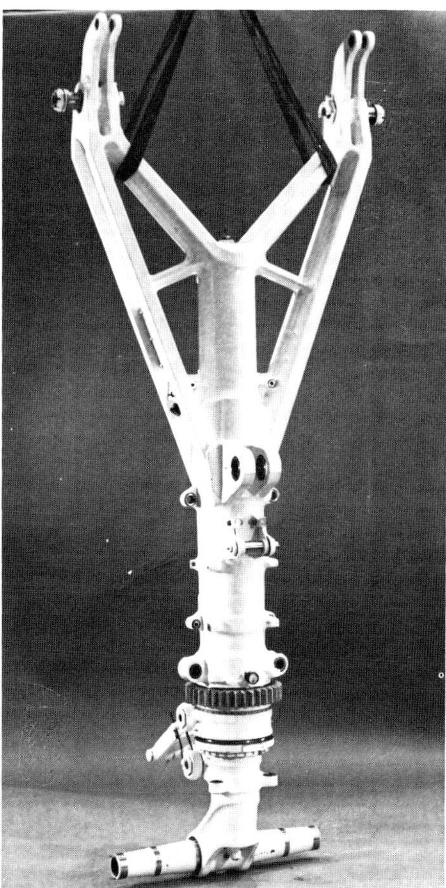

The Menasco-manufactured strut is of steel (7175-T736) and aluminum. Steering is accommodated by the ring gear on the steering collar.

B-1B NOSE LANDING GEAR

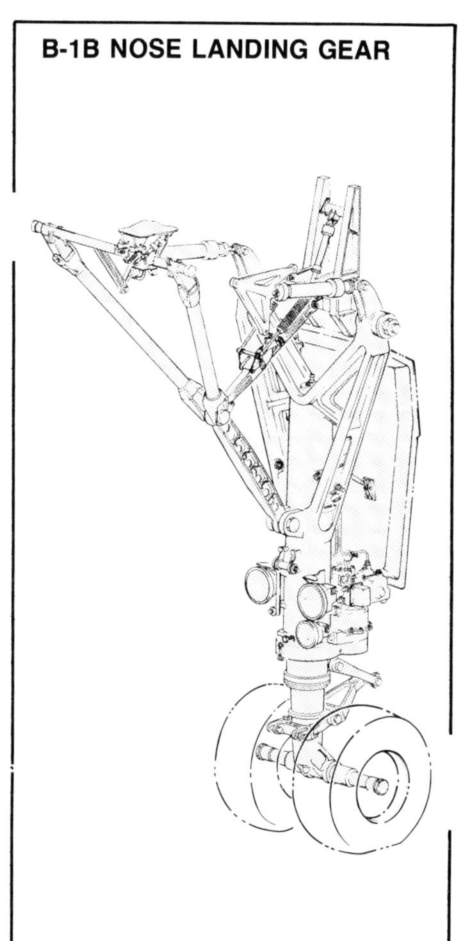

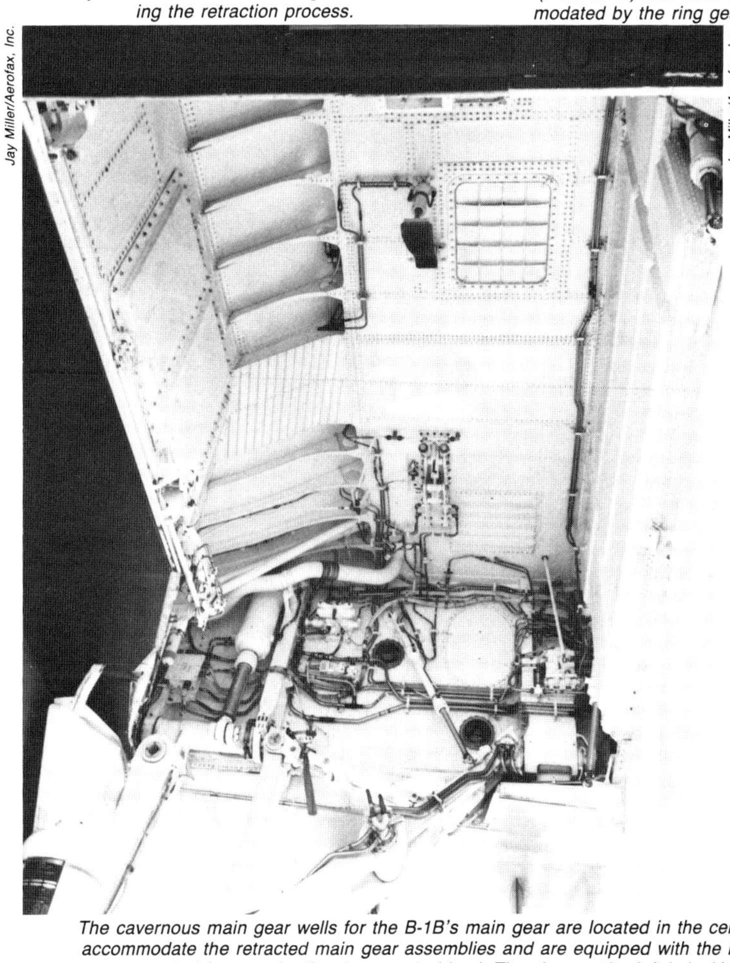

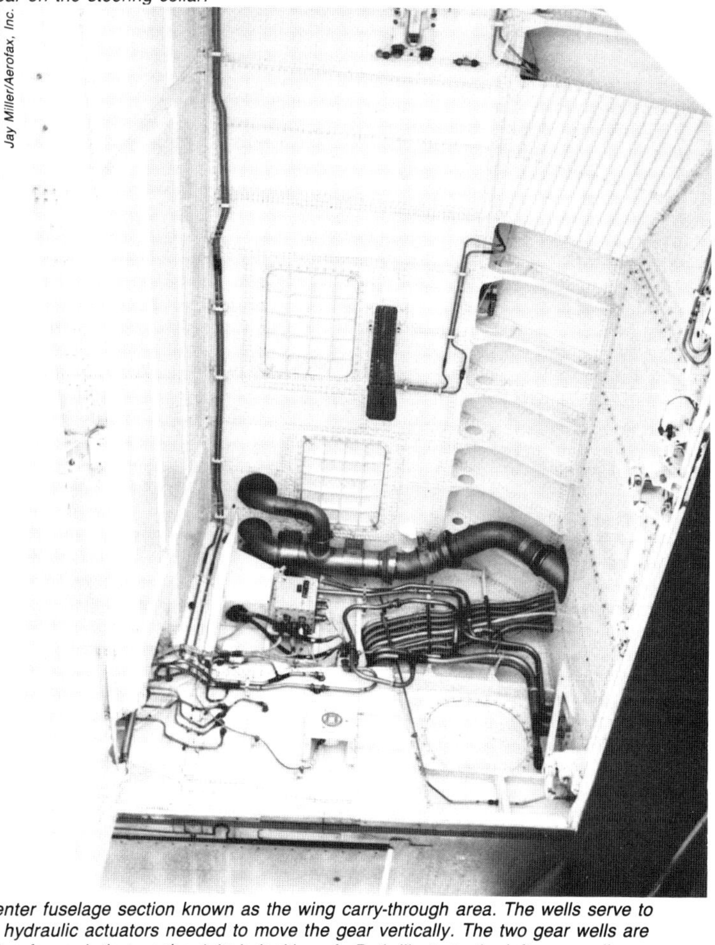

The cavernous main gear wells for the B-1B's main gear are located in the center fuselage section known as the wing carry-through area. The wells serve to accommodate the retracted main gear assemblies and are equipped with the hydraulic actuators needed to move the gear vertically. The two gear wells are separated from each other by a central keel. The view on the left is looking forward; that on the right is looking aft. Both illustrate the left gear well.

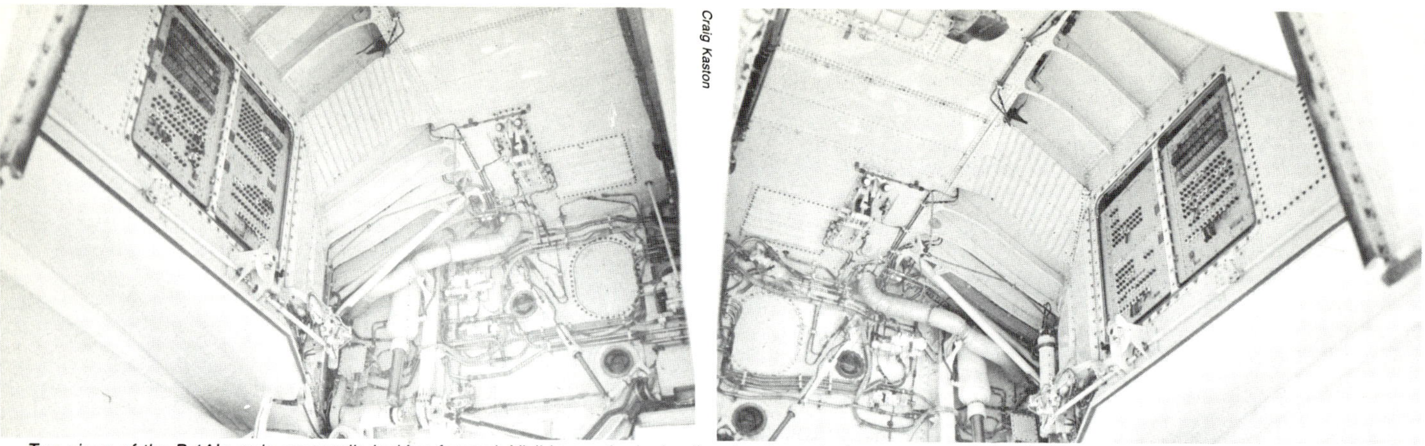

Two views of the B-1A's main gear wells looking forward. Visible are the hydraulic retraction actuators, uncovered electrical bus assemblies, and the access ports to the forward intermediate fuel tanks. Small actuators for wheel well door retraction are also visible. The main gear wells are surrounded by fuel tanks, the central and aft bomb bays, and the wing hinge support structures.

The B-1B's main gear retract rearward while working through some rather complex retraction geometries. Gear tread is relatively narrow. In this view, the gear strut fairings are readily visible, as are the extended main gear well doors. The latter normally are closed at all times except during the retraction or extension process. Down locks are visible on the door bottom edges. Proximity of the main gear to the engine nacelles is decidedly close.

The main gear strut assemblies are manufactured by Cleveland Pneumatic and are primarily of all-steel construction. Retraction and extension are accomplished through a series of hydraulic actuators which also sequentially open and close the main gear well doors. Each of the four wheels in each main gear bogie is equipped with carbon composite disc-type brakes. Each main gear, like the nose gear, is equipped with an oleo-pneumatic shock absorption unit.

The B-1A's (left) and B-1B's main gear wheels differ in detail. Besides the obvious black and white paint change, the wheel casting for the B-1A protrudes somewhat near its center, whereas that for the B-1B does not. Additionally, lug nut access holes for the B-1A are occupied and those for the B-1B are not. The main gear tires, manufactured by B.F. Goodrich, have a normal inflation pressure of between 220 and 275 lbs. per sq.''.

Front view of the B-1B main landing gear provides details of the carbon disc brake system and the main supporting strut and associated bogie. The brakes are hydraulically actuated via the rudder pedals.

The main gear well doors are opened and closed by hydraulic actuators. They are sequentially cycled so that they remain closed with the gear in either the extended or retracted position.

Rear view of left main gear provides details of oleo-pneumatic shock absorption unit and anti-torque scissor assembly.

The complex main gear strut assembly, made from machined all-steel castings is manufactured by Cleveland Pneumatic. The main center post is actually a oleo-pneumatic piston that serves as the unit's main shock-absorption unit. An anti-torque scissor prevents rotation while permitting free vertical movement.

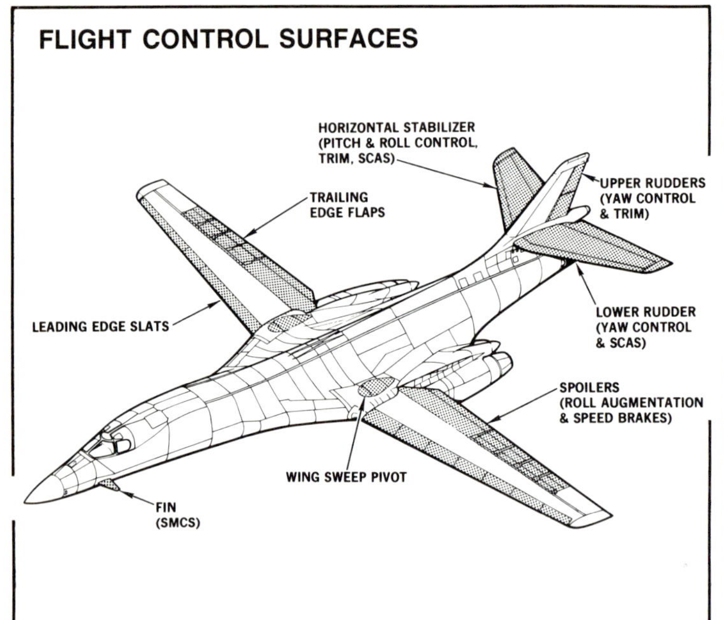

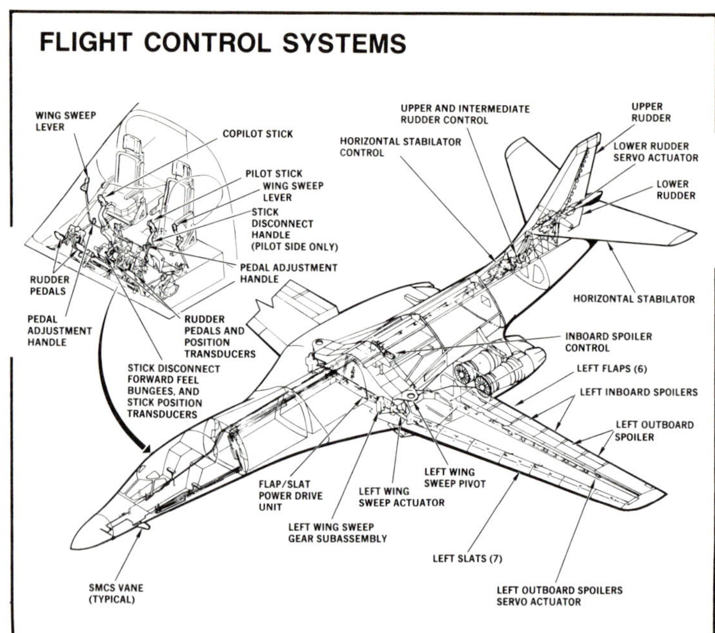

The structural mode control system (SMCS) functions to alleviate aerodynamically induced airframe stresses that can seriously shorten the aircraft's fatigue life and also, in the short term, affect crew effectiveness during a lengthy, low-altitude sorty. SMCS sensors are interfaced with several hydro-mechanical units and two nose-mounted aerodynamic vanes which serve to aerodynamically interpret the SMCS data.

The B-1B's variable sweep wing is equipped with conventional Fowler-type trailing edge flaps, and conventional leading edge slats. Both are mechanically interconnected with the wing sweep system so that inadvertent deployment does not occur when the wing is swept beyond certain angles. Both the flaps and the slats are hydro-mechanically actuated and are utilized to increase wing lift at low airspeeds.

The flaps and slats are always retracted when the wing is at its maximum sweep position. B-1A, 74-0160, illustrates the barely visible and little known wing wave guide fairing modification that was part of the Kuras-Alterman ECM package.

The B-1B's wing camber is greatly increased when both the leading edge slats and the trailing edge flaps are extended. Note the canvas-covered air-inflated rubber bladders used to seal the gap that occurs when the wings are swept.

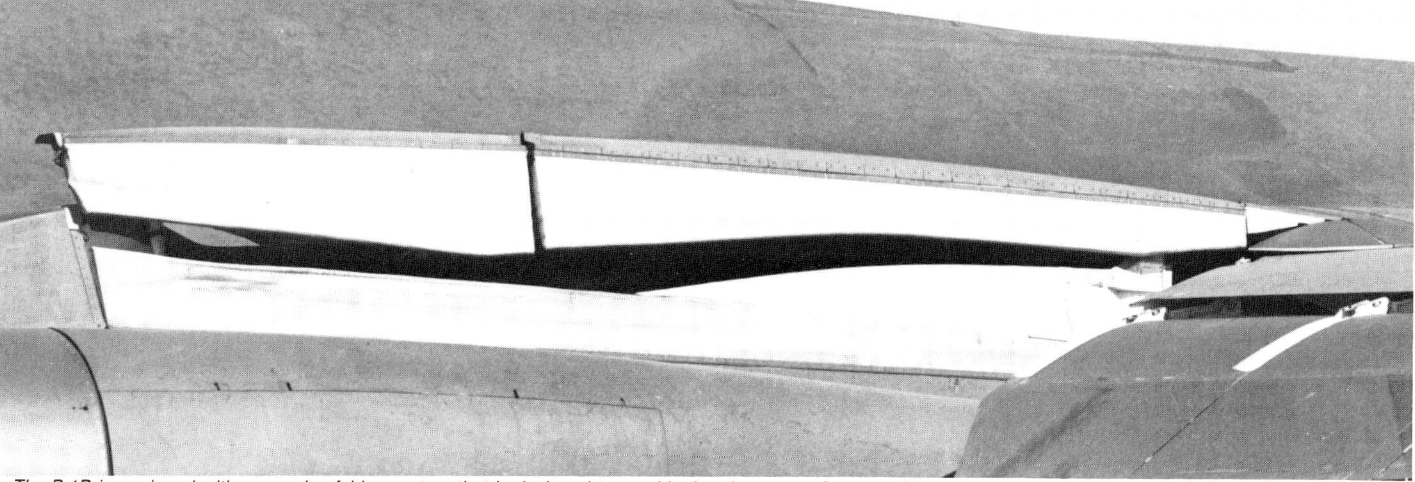

The B-1B is equipped with a complex fairing system that is designed to provide the cleanest surface transition possible where the wing trailing edge root section and engine nacelles meet during the swing sweep process. The upper fairing surface, which is hydraulically actuated, mounts a set of canvas-covered inflatable rubber bladders that serve to seal any gap that might occur when the wing is swept. A similar set of inflatable bladders fills the bottom half of the gap.

The leading edge slats are multi-segmented units interconnected to create a single movable surface. Deployment of the slats is semi-automatic and is a function of flap angle, airspeed, and wing sweep angle.

The trailing edge flaps are of the simple Fowler-type and are extended using a multiple screw-jack system. Flap extension is coordinated with wing sweep angle and involves lock-out systems that prevent sweeping with the flaps extended.

Both the B-1A (left) and B-1B are equipped with lift dumping spoilers. These units function only with the wings in their unswept position. Hydraulic actuators extend them or retract them as necessary. The B-1A spoilers were designed to be constantly extended with the aircraft sitting statically. This has been changed on the B-1B which now has spoilers that remain in the down position unless required otherwise.

The B-1B intake arrangement (left), essentially a fixed geometry design, differs from that of the B-1A in being optimized for low altitude subsonic performance and reduced radar cross section. The B-1A's intake (right) has been optimized for supersonic performance and is a variable ramp configuration permitting shock wave control as necessary. The design of the splitter assembly between each engine intake tunnel is markedly different between the B-1A and B-1B.

The aft segments of the engine nacelles and their associated fairings, as well as the engine exhaust nozzles and their associated cowls, differ greatly between the B-1A (top) and the B-1B. These changes have been dictated by aerodynamic drag studies, the revamped subsonic performance intakes of the B-1B, and radar cross section objectives. The shorter exhaust nozzles have improved powerplant performance at low altitude while lowering, slightly, the size of the i.r. plume.

Less than half the total internal volume of each engine nacelle is occupied by the engine. The rest of the nacelle consists of intake ducting and fairings for the exhaust nozzle. The reflective foil liner visible in this view is noteworthy.

The B-1B's engine nacelles feature a forward sweep to the splitter plate leading edge, and hinged vertical lips that serve to increase the capture area of the intakes at low airspeeds. The hinged lips are hydraulically actuated.

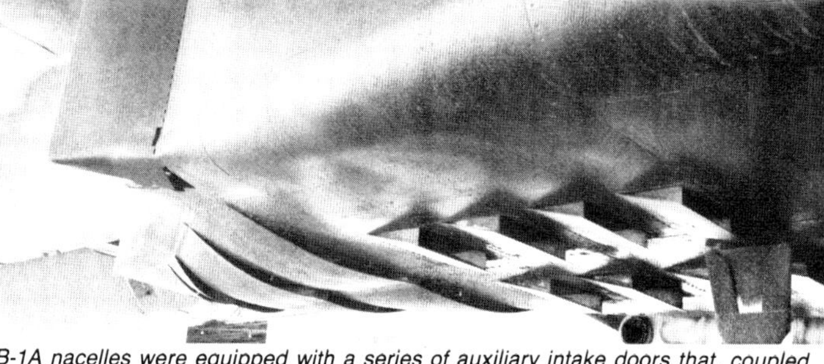

B-1A nacelles were equipped with a series of auxiliary intake doors that, coupled with the hinged vertical lips, increased the mass flow performance of the intake tunnel. FOD problems with the doors led to their elimination on the B-1B.

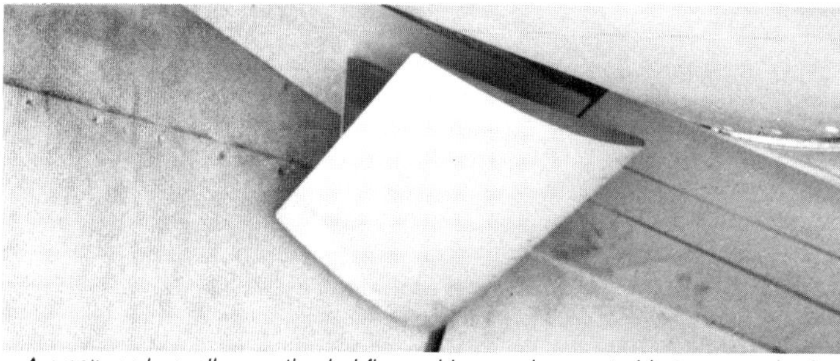

A small, and usually unnoticed airflow guide vane is mounted between each of the B-1B's engine nacelles. It serves to smooth the airflow at the aft end of the nacelle and thus improve drag characteristics and exhaust plume formation.

The B-1B's intakes are equipped with special baffle plates that significantly lower their radar reflectivity factor. Little has been revealed concerning the materials used or how the baffles function.

The auxiliary power unit exhausts for both the B-1A (shown) and B-1B are mounted between the two engines, with one being mounted in each engine nacelle. The B-1B exhaust is rectangular in cross section.

FAN SECTION   **CORE COMPRESSOR/ COMBUSTOR**   **TURBINE SECTION**   **AFTERBURNER SECTION**   **EXHAUST NOZZLE**

The General Electric F101-GE-102 augmented turbofan engine is an advanced design rated at 30,750 lbs. th. in full afterburner. It was developed specifically for use as the B-1 powerplant, though its core components are virtually identical to those found in the GE F101 DFE and the civil CFM-56 turbofans. In service, the F101-GE-102 has proven to be generally reliable, though somewhat susceptible to foreign object damage and some minor mechanical anomalies.

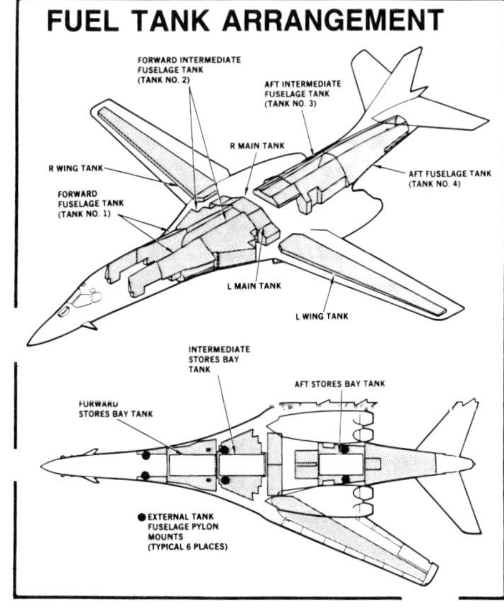

Installation of the F101-GE-102 turbofan engine is a relatively simple task facilitated by the suspended nacelle design and engineering concepts that are maintenance oriented. Though tolerances are close, the installation and removal process usually takes less than an hour.

The General Electric F101-GE-102 turbofan is relatively small for its thrust capability and is representative of state-of-the-art propulsion system design. The afterburner is short and directly attached to the exhaust nozzle. The latter is of the convergent-divergent type and provides area variations through the use of hydraulic actuators which move an actuation ring which positions the segmented flaps and seals through a series of cams and links.

The B-1B's Westinghouse AN/APQ-164 multi-mode offensive radar system is derived from the F-16C's AN/APG-68 radar. The phased array antenna is specially designed to reduce its own reflection characteristics and is optimized to provide low altitude terrain following and precise navigational functions.

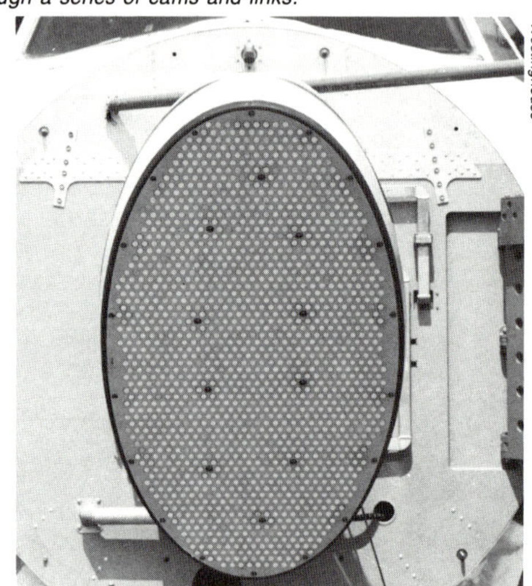

The AN/APQ-164 and its systems were tested using a modified BAC One-Eleven transport. Modifications included nose installation of the antenna.

EXCM DISPENSERS

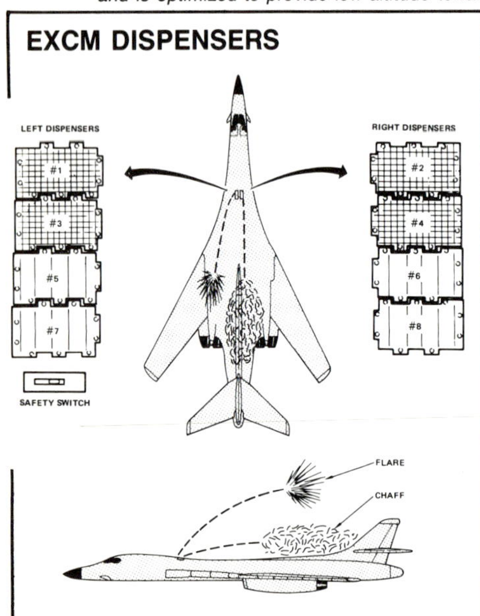

RFS/ECMS DEFENSIVE AVIONICS SYSTEM

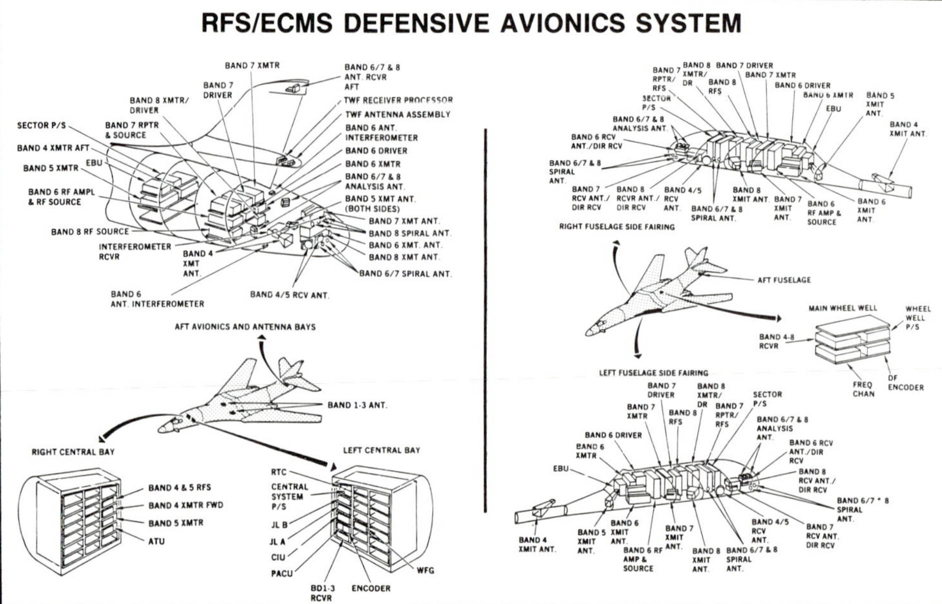

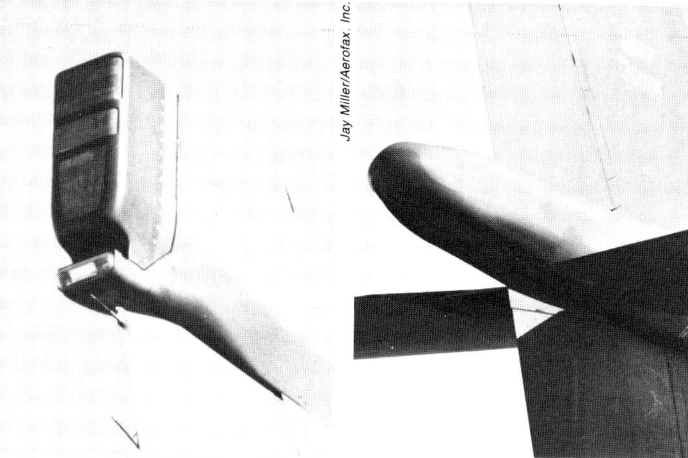

The forward fuselage section just aft of the cockpit area is a heavily blended unit that transforms the fuselage cross section from near-oval to near-triangular. It contains fuel tanks, a bomb bay, and miscellaneous avionics compartments.

Aft quadrant AN/ALQ-161 receiving antennas are mounted in the vertical fin cap fairing along with a strobe. The rear half of the horizontal stabilator vertical fin fairing accommodates additional RFS/ECM antennas and a receiver processor.

B-1A's, such as 74-0159 (left) and 76-0174, have flown with a variety of vertical fin cap and tail cone configurations. The original tail cone is seen on 74-0159, while 76-0174 is seen with the cone that would eventually be found on the production B-1B. The original cone was designed to accommodate aerodynamic requirements; the B-1B cone was designed to accommodate internally-mounted sensors.

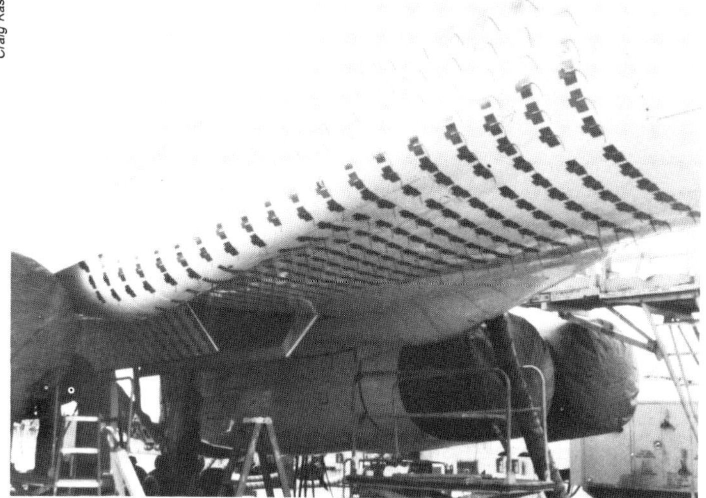

The B-1B tail cone serves as an aft mounting point for various RFS ECMS defensive system antennas. Visible in this view are several of the externally mounted antennas, and the vortex generators common to all B-1B's.

B-1A, 74-0158, was modified mid-way through its flight test program to accommodate "flow pod mod" fairings on each side of the aft bomb bay. These were designed to define and smooth the airflow around the aft bomb bay area.

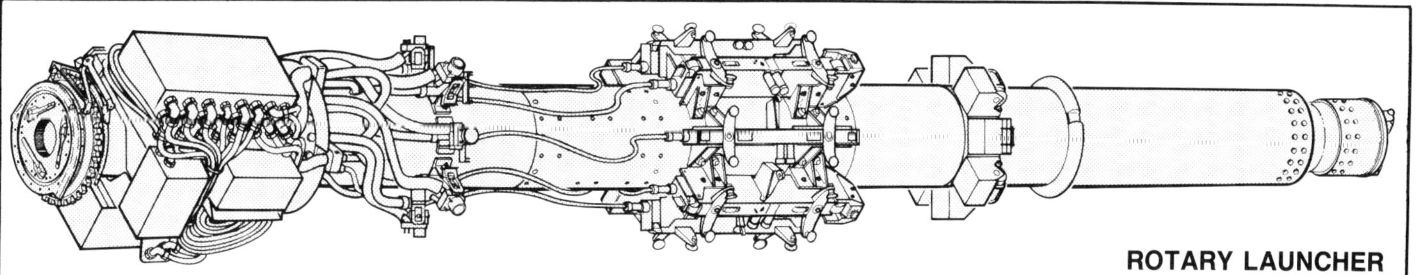

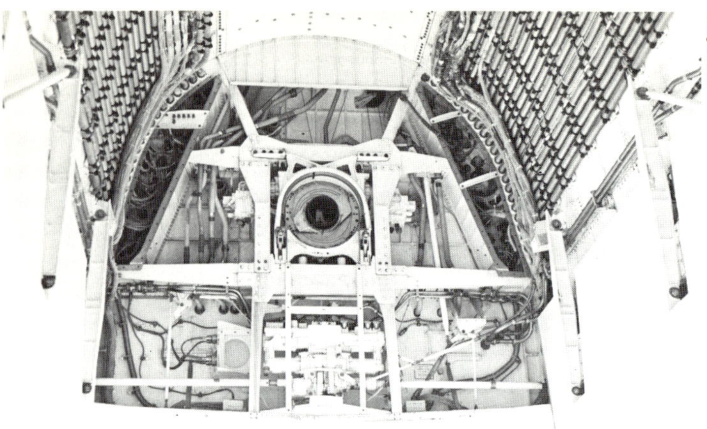

View looking forward inside the forward bomb bay of B-1A, 76-0174. The rotary launcher drive system is visible in the center of the photograph.

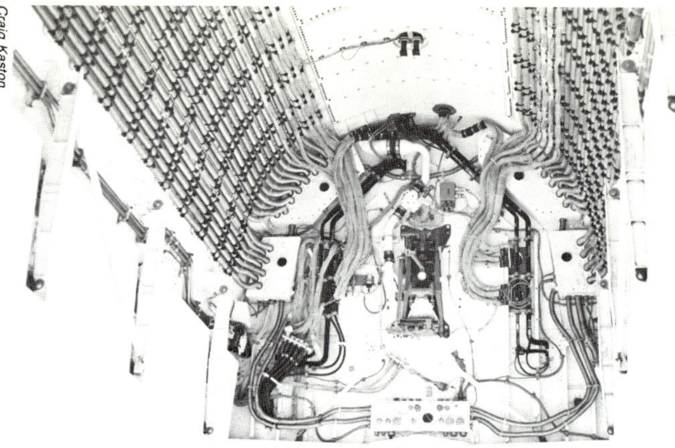

View looking aft inside the forward bomb bay of B-1A, 76-0174. Electrical harness assemblies occupy most of the interior wall space.

View looking forward inside the center bomb bay of B-1A, 76-0174. Routing of electrical harness assemblies continues through this bay.

View looking aft inside the center bomb bay of B-1A, 76-0174. The bomb bays of the B-1B remain sensitive due to their containing waveguides.

View looking forward inside the aft bomb bay of B-1A, 76-0174. The electrical harnesses are relatively few in number in this bay.

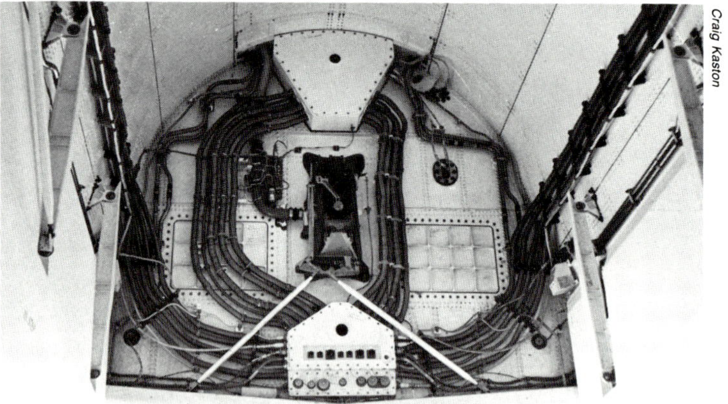

View looking aft inside the aft bomb bay of B-1A, 76-0174. Harness assemblies are attached to the aft wall in this bay and routed to the tail cone.

B-1A, 74-0159, is seen with its number two bomb bay doors partially open for SRAM deployment. Visible is the retractable spoiler installed to alleviate difficulties with bomb bay acoustics.

The bomb bay doors are of graphite composite construction with metal hardware installed at hinge points and hydraulic actuation ram connection points.